GOD OF THE EXERCISES

A Director's Diary-Directory during the Spiritual Exercises of Thirty Days

GOD OF THE EXERCISES

A Director's Diary-Directory during
the Spiritual Exercises of Thirty Days

A. Paul Dominic, SJ

GRACEWING

First published in India in 2016 by Asian Trading Corporation

This edition published in England in 2017
by
Gracewing
2 Southern Avenue
Leominster
Herefordshire HR6 0QF
United Kingdom
www.gracewing.co.uk

ISBN 978 085244 920 2

Original typesetting by Asian Trading Corporation

Cover design by Bernardita Peña Hurtado

To
Every Mother of Jesuit sons
Who could be given the title 'Mother of the Society of Jesus'
In the spirit of St Ignatius*
And also to
Every proud Father of Jesuit sons
And in particular to
My mother and father
R. Arokiam and A. Arokiam
Who shared among other things
their first name Arokiam
and their love for the Society

* He wrote to the Jesuit Antonio de Cordoba's mother Catherine of Cordoba who for all her fondness for her son was proud of his vocation: "It is not always the way of mothers to appreciate a blessing of this kind in their sons. Divine grace must be deeply working in and imprinted on your Ladyship's heart, enabling you to appreciate and love eternal good things."
On mothers like her Ignatius bestowed the title:
"Mother of the Society of Jesus."
See Hugo Rahner, *St Ignatius Loyola: Letters to Women* (Freiburg: Herder; Edinburgh–London: Nelson, 1960), pp. 381, 386.

CONTENTS

ACKNOWLEDGMENTS

Writing this book has been an exercise with the purpose of helping souls (*ayudar las animas*), which incidentally is more grand than it sounds.[1] In the process I have been helped myself by many. "What do you have that you did not receive? And if you received it, why do you boast as if it were not a gift?" (1 Cor 4:7, NRSV). The Word of God has the primacy of place in this regard. Though I have chosen different translations here and there as indicated, *I have used mostly NRSV* which is why it is not indicated regularly. Also, the words of men from St Ignatius through his generation to the present generation of Jesuits have shaped my meditative writing. The Jesuits I have lived with have also stamped my living, despite the *Sandanam* syndrome of some. Words of men (like St Thomas More) and women (like St Catherine of Siena) from the larger society of Jesus have also, to my pleasure, echoed the *Spiritual Exercises* and brought them alive to me.

Confirming me in this acknowledgment of the enduring past comes the Foreword to this book by Joseph A. Munitiz, S.J., a Past Master of Campion Hall, Oxford. With his knowledge of Ignatian sources and studies[2] he points out what or whatever I have attempted in the book. That itself is a great reward for me.

Another reward of the same kind is the Afterword by Nancy Y. Sheridan SASV who has been involved in directing the Spiritual Exercises of St Ignatius for over twenty years. Though unknown to me personally she has graciously obliged me with her attractive Afterword.

---

[1] See Suarez, *De Religione Societatis Jesu* as in H. Rahner. *The Spirituality of St Ignatius Loyola* (Chicago: Loyola University Press: 1980), pp. 104–105.

[2] See www.campion.ox.ac.uk/sites/default/files/Joe-Munitiz-Publications.pdf.

A reward though not of the same kind comes from some—in particular Sisters Innamma, Zita and Fatima—who may not be versed in St Ignatius but who draw inspiration from his tradition and encouraged me in reflecting it in my life and work.

FOREWORD

The key that opened up for Ignatius the whole world of the spiritual life can be found in one word: "reflection". It was as he lay on his sick-bed that he began to *reflect* on what was going on inside him, not on the physical level, but on another deeper level, the level of "thoughts". As he describes in his autobiography, "Our Lord was helping him, causing other thoughts." Later, in the *Spiritual Exercises*, he was to insist on the role of "recapitulation" and self-examination. It is important to *remember* the graces that one has received. And to help him do this, Ignatius himself would put them down on paper. During certain periods of his life he kept a detailed "diary", though this might be better described as a "logbook" : it served to chart the course of a journey.

The book that Paul Dominic gives us here fits snugly into this Ignatian tradition. It has much in common with the *Memoriale* of one of his heroes, the newly canonised Saint Peter Favre. It is not intended as a practical "directory", as it is far too personal. Rather it is a "diary" which introduces the reader into the spiritual world of one particular person. However, a remarkable feature of these thoughts is the wealth of references that serves to support them. To some extent, Paul Dominic is standing on the shoulders of giants: he has read and assimilated the work of most of the great modern commentators of the *Exercises*, such as the two Rahner brothers; but he acknowledges his debt to many others, including Blaise Pascal, the Anglican Longridge and he draws upon Edouard Pousset's great introduction to the spiritual life. Also very present here are such saintly figures as Thomas More and John Climacus. The Indian context is an especially strong feature of this book, partly from the use of Hindu terms and partly from an appreciation of what devout Hindus can teach us.

But the fascination of this text for me personally was that it allowed me to follow the progress of this "director" as he grows in knowledge of his own weakness and dependence on the One who really directs. *To contemplate meant for me for so very long to imagine the scene and exercise my powers of imagination to the details of the scene and of course with faith being active. But recently, Lord, I learned that it is far more than that and I became aware of the deeper currents of contemplative exercise.* He has to come to realize that *spiritual fireworks* - a phrase that recurs more than once and includes *sensible consolation or élan or contrived spiritual euphoria* - are not what all this is about. It may not be a bad sign to feel *cut off from You.* Thus he can write, *I ought not, dare not, assume the over-all responsibility for the retreat.* Paul Dominic's dialogue is with the God of the *Exercises,* who takes the form of loving Father, faithful Son and ever-helpful female Spirit. Here one senses a deep affection that can overcome any *sense of inability or ineptitude, at other times haunted by a mood of uselessness and even dread.*

There is much to be learned from 'The God of the Exercises', because it demonstrates, through one man's personal experience, what in practice the giving of the *Exercises* entails. The paradox lies in that (as Ignatius instructs in one of the directories that he dictated) "He who gives the Exercises should take care to contribute nothing of his own beyond the ministry of giving the Exercises." And yet the honesty of "the one who gives" is indispensable. Paul Dominic's account shows the need both of this self-effacement and of this honesty.

Joseph A. Munitiz, S.J.
Former Master of Campion Hall, Oxford

INTRODUCTION

The term Directory in Jesuit history is a set of directives about the manner of giving the Spiritual Exercises. More than one of them derive from St Ignatius himself! In the Directory dictated by him to Fr Juan Alonso de Vitorio, the ninth directive reads: "He (the giver of the Exercises) should take care to contribute nothing of his own beyond the ministry of giving the Exercises... with a great deal of charity, concern and prayer. He should beseech God earnestly on the exercitant's behalf not to allow this soul to be led astray because of the sins of the one giving him the Exercises."[1] What is presumed in this directive is that the director has made the Exercises and imbibed them.

This does not seem to be obvious in the directive found in the Short Instruction probably from Father Everard Mercurian, the fourth General of the Jesuits (1573-1580). There was already the need to insist: "The director should meditate on the Exercises he is about to give, and ask the Lord Jesus for grace of picking out as well as possible from what he has meditated the most helpful things to say to the exercitant." This insistence is reinforced almost immediately thus: "For correctly giving the Exercises to others the most essential thing is for one to have previously made and thoroughly meditated them himself, and then re-meditate them just before giving them."[2]

In the Directory of Juan Alfonso de Polanco a lengthy directive suggests how the director should, in general, take care that he prepares himself along with the exercitants to cooperate fully with God's grace. "For this," as the directive explains, "it will help if the director desires with ardent charity to see the exercitant's salvation and spiritual progress for the sake of God's glory and out of a wish to see God's will accomplished in the exercitant, as perfectly as possible. It will also help if the director, recognizing that while of his own power he is unable to produce this supernatural operation of grace in the exercitant he is nevertheless able to obtain this power from the infinite goodness of God and cooperate with it, will earnestly pray for the exercitant throughout the Exercises, remembering him in his Masses, particularly at moments of special need. He should beg the prayers of others as well."[3]

A short and simple directive, reminiscent of Mercurian, and associated with Fabio de Fabi enjoins on the director: "Before giving each meditation he should spend some time pondering it himself."[4]

The Directory of Gil González Dávila envisages the director "meditating beforehand what he will say and commending to God in prayer," so that in this way "the hearer's mind will be fired and better disposed for prayer."[5]

All the above directives find their place in some way in the official *Directory to the Spiritual Exercises*. Here is one example: "It will be well also that the director should, if possible, spend a little time in meditating upon each Exercise himself before giving it, in order that he may impress it more forcibly upon the exercitant."[6] Another directive suggests that "he ought ... to help them (exercitants) with his own prayers."[7]

The *Granada Directory* has a counsel which no director can ignore. "Whoever desires to give the Exercises to others should be fully imbued with the unction of the Holy Spirit; that is to say, the Holy Ghost is to be the primary instructor, for the giver and the maker of the Exercises." With such faith, however, goes sustained experience and skill. "The one who gives the Exercises must be able to discriminate between the motions of the various spirits, be able to apply the discernment of spirits (that is, have

2

long experience in meditating on the Spiritual Exercises), and possess a special skill in the spiritual guidance of souls." Who can be equal to such requirements? "Whoever is not endowed with these gifts must, at the minimum, make a thorough study of the Exercises and then pray from the bottom of his heart that God may deign to supply what is lacking to him."[8]

Three important demands are made of the directors as they engage in giving the Exercises. They need to pray for themselves; next, they themselves should meditate on the matter of the Exercises in the very course of a one-month retreat; and thirdly, they must intercede for their exercitants as they accompany them all through the retreat. Only to the extent that they carry out these activities behind the scenes they will succeed in staging "the Divine Comedy of the *Exercises*"[9] for their exercitants. In the very doing of their bounden duty they let God pour out into the empty vessels of their prayerful reflection the bitter-sweet water of grace[10] according to their varying need.

What follows is an exercise in fulfilling the triple demands as I was privileged to conduct the long retreat to souls of various hues, many of whom made the Exercises far better than I did for the first time or second time or even third time. When I first felt drawn to jot down the diary of my praying during the time I gave the Exercises, I did a sort of meditative writing on the matter of the Exercises; that corresponded, as I was surprised to find later, to one of the suggestions of the earliest official Directory. Surprised all the more by my other two findings in the Directories regarding the director's praying during the Exercises, I felt drawn in course of time to implement the other two purposes of praying, namely for myself and for the retreatants.

I wish that in these prayers there had been, in the best Jesuit tradition, "a truly experiential knowledge of God, a contact with God which far surpasses all merely intellectual cognition... knowledge 'through action', a prayerful sense of what is *for* God and what *against* him." But I'm afraid I was trying to be "devout only through speculation."[11] Whatever purpose it may serve or not in the future, it served me as a small search for God's ways of dealing with souls, including mine! Taking all this into consideration, I believe that this spiritual diary of mine, as an accompanist of the Exercises, is drawn from the books of the Bible along with the *Spiritual Exercises* and their commentaries, and my own life-book of interior experience, and also hopefully the unction of the Holy Spirit. If I present this to the public it is in the spirit of what Jerome Nadal advocated following St Ignatius: "It is not sufficient that a person should grasp the things of God, even if he does so in virtue of a gift infused by God, but it is necessary that he should proclaim what he has learnt *in facie Ecclesiae.*"[12]

I believe that all good directors of the Exercises—which is not to say, the famous or much demanded ones—have done the triple directorial prayer-tasks either spontaneously or deliberately. Whenever they pray deliberately in the humble consciousness of their responsibility they ward off unsuspected intrusion of selfishness in their ministry and make their intention pure enough to become an *instrumentum conjunctum cum Deo* (an instrument conjoined to God), to use an expression of St Ignatius.[13] In this respect it is worth quoting from the old Counsels of Father Duarte Pereyra regarding the immediate preparation of a would-be director. "For this it would be good for him to try hard to have a right intention in this ministry, desiring or seeking therein nothing except what is for the greater honour and glory of the Lord and the greater good of the person's soul.... (For this) he should place no reliance upon himself or upon his own strength and efforts, but great reliance upon the Lord and upon the special help which God promised the members of the Society for carrying their ministries. The grace of religion is a special help and concursus of God for carrying out the ministries of the order, and particularly this ministry, just as we have seen and every day continue to see how much our Lord has worked in souls through this means."[14]

What struck me in my recent serendipitous discoveries on this matter is the appreciation of the directors' praying for themselves and the retreatants. Joseph Veale has not thought it exaggerating to claim: "It is part of the incomprehensible dynamic of the Exercises that the Spirit works through the prayerful relationship of the director and the retreatant."[15] And Brian Grogan has not thought it trivial to urge sustained intercession which any concerned Christian can do for another: "The retreat-giver who has a right sense of order, that is, a sense of the primacy of God in the whole enterprise of the retreat, will spend much time interceding with the Lord for the retreatant."[16] And indeed doing something more, namely thanksgiving, which runs through the whole gamut of the Exercises in its various melodies and nuances. If St Ignatius owed this direction regarding thanksgiving to several sources, not the least is *The Imitation of Christ*. And therefore it is no surprise to come upon these words of Christ: "Return the greatest thanks to the Divine Goodness, which deals so favourably with you, which mercifully visits you, ardently incites you, and powerfully raises you up; lest by your own weight you fall down to the things of the earth."[17]

LOOKING TOWARDS THE EXERCISES

I was ready to be sought out by those who did not ask,
to be found by those who did not seek Me.
I said, 'Here I am, here I am',
to a nation that did not call on My name. (Is 65:1)[18]
He who has prepared us for this very thing is God;
He has given us the Spirit as a guarantee. (2 Cor 5:5)

"My beloved, I'll do everything for you."
"The hearing of this, Your word, is enough to comfort my heart!"
"At the same time, My beloved, I want you
to do everything to help yourself!"
"Doesn't it mean, Rabbuni, You'll help me every day
to do all the good that I can by myself?
It'll be such an assurance for me
that You will do all You want for me in Your goodness
for the simple reason that it is beyond me!"

"You will succeed, not by your own strength, but by My spirit.
Obstacles as great as mountains will disappear before you. You
will rebuild the Temple, and as you put the last stone in place, the
people will shout, 'Beautiful, beautiful!'" (Zech 4:6-7, GNB)

I know, "One who is indisposed to receive a favour, deserves to
be deprived of it." So said one of your saintly saints, Peter Faber,
one who had the approbation of Ignatius for his way of giving the
Exercises! And so, as I look towards the Exercises I'd like to wait
on You, hoping for a *darshan* of You that will serve Your purposes.
I'd dispose myself thinking of You, looking at You, listening to
You, etc. I'd like to be in the company of the exercitants' angels
and saints who are continually in Your presence, enjoying eternal

6

darshan. With them and after them I pray: "My heart is ready, O God; my heart is ready" (Ps 57:7).

Yes, how good it is to realize "The readiness is all!"[19] so that I may come to rejoice at the end, "Ripeness is all!"[20] I believe heartily: "God never refuses that first grace that gives one the courage to act; afterwards the heart is strengthened and one advances from victory to victory."[21] So may I cherish with vigilance "the work of salvation ceaselessly performed in our inmost being with all the skill and sweetness of the Holy Spirit's artistry"? With such sentiments we begin our *peregrinatio in stabilitate* – pilgrimage without moving,[22] looking to "this heaven-sent Director, who can teach us all things ... (who will) never find us unprepared when He comes but always with faces uplifted and hearts expanded to receive the copious blessing".[23]

Dear Jesus, as I keep watch, "Let me hear what God the Lord will speak, for He will speak peace to His people, to His faithful, to those who turn to Him in their hearts." (Ps 85:8)

Thinking of what You, Lord God, could do in me for the retreat

I recall "Loyola's epitaph": "*Non coerceri maximo, contineri tamen a minimo divinum est.*" Did Ignatius get You right, Lord? And did that zealous but anonymous Flemish Jesuit get you right, Jesus? "To suffer no restriction from anything, however great, and yet to be contained in the tiniest of things—that is divine." This is the simple claim, dear Jesus, or bold vaunt I flourish for expecting great things from You for the retreat! Though I feel I'm neither greatest nor tiniest still I've my illusions about my greatness and delusions about my smallness. Such a wrong self-image of superiority or inferiority complex does not serve You best for Your work in me and through me for the sake of the retreatants. Yet I believe in Your sovereignty in dealing with persons! On the one hand, You will not be hampered in Your work by my persona of ego exaltation; and on the other, You will be willing to abide even in my minimized self and reveal Yourself to others even through or beyond my own self-caricature.

Will not this very sovereign and sublime way of Yours, Lord, make me, in spite of whatever I am, less unworthy of You and more truthful to You? In what other way, Lord, can I make myself a useful and pliable instrument in Your hands? *Instrumentum conjunctum cum Deo*—can anyone be greater than this, however great one is? In the case of one who is small, the greater the smallness the greater will be the power released through one!

Thinking of my need of relating to the exercitants

I thank you, Abba, Lord God of all the living, for the exercitants – the *sadhaks* – who will be coming to make the Exercises. I don't know them nor do they know me; but You know them as well as me. It is You who have given them to me and I want to be with them and them to be with me where and how and how long You choose! If I have to deal with them it cannot be without a certain savoir-faire or social favour. Whether it is a gift inborn in me or acquired as an art by me, I want something—whatever the name for it—more pleasant and efficacious and guaranteed. How else except as "taught only by the unction of the Holy Spirit (1 Jn 2:20, 27) and by the prudence which God our Lord communicates to those who trust in His Divine Majesty?"[24]

With whatever share of grace that is mine I'll wait on You and watch Your dealings with each one of Your chosen ones, the exercitants. Especially in my ignorance of what is going to happen during the retreat in them and for them, I'll constantly remember that You are the real Director who is ever in command, despite our freedom, which sadly means, more often than not, weak or wanton movements or meanderings. So I gladly wait to pick up every clue of guidance from You. After all, You've assured Your progeny from time immemorial that we are not to seek You in vain.

So I shall learn what I should have long ago done ... reverence in the presence and action in me and around me of Your divine Majesty! To run after You and not ahead of You in my dealings with the exercitants so that they will feel assured that, whatever I do, I do not do on my own but with You, relying on You![25] I like to think that the time of the Exercises is time of labour and birth: "a supernatural birth in which pain and travail and involuntary sadness are experienced; these are liable from time to time to torment both parent and offspring and to stifle them, unless a conscientious and experienced midwife is present, and especially light from heaven, and strength and perception from above."[26] As the exercitants cannot escape their labour may I not fail to assist them in their hour of need, following Your past intervention and present inspiration.

Thinking of the Exercises

Your will is our sanctification and Your boundless goodness is always ready to pour out – indeed is actually pouring out – Your gifts upon all Your creatures; and, of course, how much more so on us Your rationally privileged creation. Without doubt therefore I believe this: if anyone interposes no impediment, but rather brings the right dispositions, one will easily and in a short time obtain great graces from You.[27] Life favours the prepared mind, they say; and You are Life, the Life indeed! The Spiritual Exercises, as I come to recognize more and more, propose an experienced way of readying oneself for the uttermost graces necessary for life, life that is You. I pray therefore that everyone of the retreatants may experience this through the Exercises just as Your chosen servant Ignatius did, led primarily by You, led ultimately by none other than You.

I wish I could add "just as I myself did experience," thanks to Your all-embracing and all-enabling grace! After all, am I not to be an objective norm for the exercitants who are trying and seeking to determine the will of God for themselves? This means, among other things, that I must be free and at peace with myself. I cannot therefore let myself be worked up and become excessively elated or disturbed, but must steadily accompany and, when necessary, direct my client-seeker to a deeper level of discernment.[28] Knowing however my poverty of discernment I ask for Your wisdom, for the exercise of whatever wisdom You have imparted to me ... and will still impart to me. I ask so especially because of the gracious way of Yours in relation to Solomon when he asked for wisdom; and much more especially because of the assurance of Your gift of the Spirit by Your Son, the One greater than Solomon. So You'll guard me— won't You, Lord?—from exhaustion of my mere human determination so that I will find in myself certain inner strength to receive Your prevenient grace and do the actual work here and now.

Lord, the retreatants I'll be having are Yours, and You know them and their dispositions and desires and designs. I don't know them; but I know how they should be ideally inclined. If only they could enter the retreat "not so much in order to enjoy spiritual sweetness"[29] but learn Your will concerning them (# 1.4)![30] As You should enable them in this regard, may I see for myself that Your will itself is our peace (as Dante felt) and even more, yes, our spiritual sweetness. While I can't but wish that I were "well versed in spiritual things and especially in these Exercises"[31] equally I can't but feel something of all that I lack in this respect. But one thing I'm sure of: You are all versed in my things and in those of the retreatants; and You can sort them out for us. That certainty should be enough for me! Whatever You do, I believe, will help us to help ourselves (# 1.1)[32] and to help one another.

Lead us, then, Lord, through the itinerary of the Exercises. With You each one of us will pass through the major stages of the Christian Exodus experience. At each stage of the maze of the Exercises we shall with Your help discern, and hopefully choose to want what You Yourself want of us, not for Yourself but for ourselves.[33] In all this testing time and space of the Holy Spirit may we not be found wanting! Or is it more proper to say that in all this exhibition of Your favour may we not be found wanting in fervour? Is it not through our fervour that You contact us and keep us close to Yourself and even come to contain us?

I recall now a caution I read somewhere. Physical contact can be made without any special preparation but not so spiritual contact which needs no small preparation because it is a very subtle phenomenon. For example, like a small, slight breeze coming in that, if we are not aware, we will not be able to feel.[34] However true it may sound, Lord, I believe Your functioning in us goes beyond our normal functioning or readiness or preparedness! For I believe it is You, for Your own loving purpose, who put both the will and action in us (Ph 2:13). So I give glory to You whose power working in us, can do infinitely far more than we ask or imagine (Eph 3:20). And this, all through the labyrinth of the Exercises till we reach the Centre.

"Yes, My beloved, you are right: 'only the unction of the Holy Spirit and the prudence which the Lord imparts to those who trust His divine majesty ultimately teaches the true way.'[35] Well begun thus is well ended!"

1. JESUS! YESHŪA!

The Spirit searches everything, even the depths of God.
For what human being knows what is truly human
except the human spirit that is within?
So also no one comprehends what is truly God's
except the Spirit of God.
Now we have received not the spirit of the world,
but the Spirit that is from God,
so that we may understand the gifts
bestowed on us by God. (1 Cor 2:10-12)

"If only you knew the grace of God ..."
"Oh, yes, won't You, then, Rabbuni, help me this day
to do by myself all the good that You inspire me to do?
It'll be an assurance for me
that You will do all You want for me in Your goodness
for the simple reason that You can't do otherwise!"

Eve of the retreat

Dear Jesus, may I call You so? I ask You so, because I feel far from You on account of a particular experience of block or backlog which You know better than I do. It is worse than a thorn in my side. But trusting and knowing that You are not far from me on Your part I cannot bring myself to address You in an impersonal way. And so I dare to belong ... following Ignatius! Will this sense of belonging be deeper if I call You as Your mother or father called You in Aramaic: YESHŪA?

It cannot be without Your inspiration that St Ignatius placed your name (in the diminutive form IHS) as a caption at the beginning of his *Spiritual Exercises*. I take it as an invitation to us to be infused with the love of Your Name; and so right at the start the exercitants and I make an option for Jesus in all that pertains to life and, in particular, to giving and making the Exercises. I hope that such an appropriation of Jesus will hopefully lead to the making of new life for all of us concerned so that we will become living monograms of Jesus.

My Jesus, I believe You've chosen me this time to direct these chosen ones who are going to do their Spiritual Exercises. I didn't seek them out; they came to me; indeed they were sent to me. So I believe, however much I may be unprepared for it, You want me to lead them through the Spiritual Exercises.... Shall I be able to help them thus? With all my heart, Lord, I hope so. Even so, I've no pretension of helping others! Maybe "I shall merely try to help God as best I can," as an unusual Jewess told herself even in distress all around. Or better still, I'll just stand by You, my God; "and if I succeed in doing that, then I shall be of use to others as well. But I mustn't have heroic illusions about that either."[36] That is not to say, however, I've no hopes; on the contrary I have desires and hopes Himalayan high, as urged by Your stalwart protagonists like Ignatius (## 5.1-2; 15.3-6) and Teresa of Avila.

For, the fact that, at this moment, I can say I want to stand by You means and foreshadows something good; doesn't it, my good Lord God? Can't I be confident and proud that You have led me to Yourself in some real way? A way that I may be surprised to discover later as nothing less than extraordinary! All Your ways, whatever they may be, are they not extraordinary?... And so I look for "the highest grace and everlasting love"[37] of Yours to accompany me and Your exercitants.

Anyway, Lord, what You have done to me You had done earlier, of course, in unique, paradigmatic ways to countless others like Ignatius. I'd like to conduct myself like him who could not but share his discovery of God with anyone interested; I'd like to act in my small, hopefully Spartan, Manresan way of conversion, using the very means he used with extraordinary results—the Spiritual Exercises. You had helped him to devise the Exercises as a help for that very purpose. Knowing their effectiveness and power, some were convinced that the Exercises came, if I may say so, straight from You, Christ Jesus, my Lord![38]

> O Lord, I have heard of Your renown,
> and I stand in awe, O Lord, of Your work.
> In our own time revive it;
> in our own time make it known. (Hab 3:2)

Trusting in the same kind of help I employ the same means, hoping to attain the same end. May the exercitants then come to have a feel of Your reality concretely in their lives through the Exercises. This is what I shall present and offer the retreatants in and through the Spiritual Exercises: nothing less than an immediate encounter with You. As I say this—whether boldly or rashly, You know it, Lord—I almost can't believe myself. I believe, yet I add, "Help my unbelief," as You believe in people, all people, including me, struggling with belief and unbelief!

At the same time, Counsellor God, may I fail to do harm even with good intention! Not like the Jesuit *peritus* at Vatican II who took into his head to thrust on me his psychological diversion when all I wanted was his declaration of Your forgiveness in the sacrament of penance during a retreat! God forbid! There are spiritual counsellors who want to guide their clients according to their counsel alone, thinking what is good for them is so for others too,[39] and in the process becoming prey to changing ideals that offer neither foundation nor integration. Let me learn to do according to Your counsel, as You alone, Lord, can see our souls and read our hearts and know our moods. Therefore, while offering the retreatants the blessed assurance that they too can come to know God personally through the Spiritual Exercises let me seek Your counsel regarding Your particular approach and action in each one of them! If there are skills to facilitate the immediate experience (*anubhava*) of You in the retreatants, let me go beyond the technique of the skills ... let me experience and exude their art and spirit. Surely no skill can be like the spiritual skill, the skill that Your Spirit communicates even to me when She moves in me for the sake of others. Like Her in her attractive art of life-movement may I move with the retreatants with due reserve (due to their power of freedom) and due warmth (due to their need of human frailty) as is proper to different situations. Also, let me be observant and mindful enough of the natural gifts and qualities of the retreatants, which after all the Spirit makes use of in Her work on them. God forbid that I should be more spiritual in my ways than the Spirit. As Your grace, ever ancient and new, builds on nature with its store, not vacuum, of gifts ever evolving so may I follow suit in accompanying Your retreatants. May I assist them thus in the emergence of their interior universe! So, Abba of us all, may You prosper us all ... as I sing this song:

> We must not force the tender shoot to grow at the rhythm of impatience.
> Nor can we grab at the heart with our hands to make beat faster...
> We cannot stir the rhythm of time, wanting to mature history
> by imposing our will
> and harvesting the kingdom before the appointed hour.
> Cross the rough edges, encourage the long day, look tenderly upon insecure steps, free the imprisoned moment, and let the kingdom
> reach its height by the hand of God that holds the mystery![40]

And so I believe You never refuse the first necessary grace that enables us to start and continue so that what is well begun may be well ended! So I start with courage here and now, having no anxious thought of the coming days (## 11.1-2; 76.3).

Pondering the way

Dear Jesus, how shall I deliver the Spiritual Exercises to the exercitants? Isn't it my first duty as a retreatant-turned-retreat-director to seek and find in what way You want me to conduct the retreat? I have long heard of the conversational word of God as part of the ordinary apostolic means of Your least Society (IHS, meaning also Iesu Humilis Societas). Not long ago I was pleasantly surprised to know that the same means is also the way of imparting or communicating the Spiritual Exercises to the exercitants. Dear Jesus, open therefore my lips and they will praise You and Your name before the exercitants. This You will do authoritatively as Lord and consummately as the invariable Divine Companion, accompanying me and them.

May I receive from You, the Word, the gift of speech, the gift of passing on Your words, the gift of conversing about them with my exercitants, given our loquacious nature?

May my conversational Word of God be a real, natural conversation with them about You and Your Abba Father and Your Spirit. May this my spiritual conversation be breathed forth by the Spirit, blown by the Spirit, filled with the unction of the Spirit and so be wholly spiritual. May it, to be effective, also be a conversation – simple, natural, homely, human, down-to-earth, interesting, yes, interesting too, and absorbing, and, of course, affecting our life. Too much to ask, Lord? Why should it be so, if it is for Your greater glory? I ask this knowing that the book of the Exercises is "unemotional almost as a treatise on geometry" and yet the Exercises of the book have "set so many loving hearts on fire and filled the history of the Church with heroes"[41] and heroines who have walked Your labyrinthine ways.

May I converse with my exercitants about what You've conversed with me in recent hours and days, in past seasons, in my own Spiritual Exercises, in my waking life, in my dreaming life, in my working life, in my social life, in my drifting life and, of course, in my life with You, if at all this could be separated from the above. After all, that is how You set Ignatius on his new profession, exciting in him even a responsibility to communicate to others his new found discovery. That means experience (*anubhava*) of life with You is effectively destined to be shared. Of course my interior experience is not comparable to his. But that doesn't make it any less of an experience; does it, Lord? Again, if I may dare ask: "Is it not, at times, from quite simple experiences wherein God's presence and action are detected, that we can help others to understand how God acts in them and is actually leading them?"[42]

If I may dare say so, let me converse with them as You did with Andrew and his companion on the bank of the Jordan or with two disciples on the way to Emmaus even when they couldn't suspect it could be You talking to them? May I hope to win their confidence and warm their hearts as You did, but without too much consciousness of myself doing so? As on that occasion when Jyc was moved to share with me with clouded eyes what had thrilled her without my knowing during our meeting the previous day. As I thank You, Jesus, for that wonderful, unsolicited unction may I have many more such surprises, as You feel best of course. Would You not then make our hearts burn as You illumine the book of our life with the light of the book of Your life?

My Lord Jesus, I don't want to be anxious therefore about the so-called talks I'll be giving them, whether reading from prepared notes or from the Book of the Spiritual Exercises or inspired on the spur of the moment.

Let me rather say to them what I've to say to them as You direct me to. Let it not be wordy, bloated with words (as even Anthony of Padua was inspired to warn), but full of the Word, of Your Word, that is of Yourself and Your speech, heard in the silences as the still small voice and also in the disturbances. Lord, as the Word of God, Yours is the first word and Yours the last!

17

Let my speech be like that of Ignatius after his ten-month stay in the cave of Manresa. He felt like sharing his experience of You, he had to share it, he could not but share it with people around. You had taught him, untrained and backward as he was, like a kindly school teacher; and he began teaching others in his turn without knowing it. Such was his apprenticeship with You as the Trainer.

As You teach me—I wouldn't know how—but as You teach me in accordance with Your prophetic word (Is 54:13; Jer 31:34), may I be taught and trained to speak simply, humbly, spiritually, revealingly so that finally the exercitants know that You, the Creator, deal with them directly and so creatively (# 15.3-4). Am I then called, dear Lord, to share what I live by so that others may experience an awakening to the life of the Spirit moving in us?

May such privileged conversations with my exercitants be so real and normal that You become part of our normal human life of ordinary social intercourse. Hopefully, then, the Spiritual Exercises will become the very exercise of our life, of mine and the exercitants. You will be in our life, in our speech, in our silence, in our rest, in our sleep, and indeed in all that we shall be or do. You will be all in all, Lord. Then surely this retreat will stay its course. It surely will not unless there has been something which did not come from ourselves (because it could not come from ourselves) but which could come only from You![43] This is truly spiritual aerobics, of ours and above all of Yours.

There is something in me that makes me believe I am one of the many privileged, if only least, heirs to the great spiritual privilege bestowed on Your servant, the lesser Ignatius, a privilege that he would not trade for any other, a privilege that became a heritage for Christians, even Protestant Christians[44] of latter times. A singular heritage within the longer, larger Christian heritage. I'd like to be, in my own way, its humble, faithful guardian and so I'd like to share it further as best as I can. Then perhaps I shall,

for purposes of service, share, even speak, in masterly fashion ...
in some way like, if not exactly like, the true master. Won't You
bless me and the exercitants You have given me ... so that, with
my help, they too will come to their rightful heritage?

At night

Jesus, Lord, as I was speaking to the exercitants in my first meeting
with them, I didn't feel my conversation was appealing to them.
Certainly a picture of me so small or poor or immature or even
ill-formed. But I know enough to leave it in Your Providence. By
way of expressing this trust I recall; "No one can receive anything
except what has been given from heaven" (Jn 3:27). However in
my concern for them who look to me for help and guidance, I ask
earnestly that, where my conversation has been found wanting and
boring, Your interior conversation may carry them through, above
and forward. Lord, even as I take stock of myself in my relationship
with the exercitants I know it won't be all that beneficial unless
You take me by hand and lead me.

My only desire, Lord, is to tell the retreatants about You, Your love
and grace, and about Your Son Jesus Christ, Crucified and Risen,
and about Your Spirit, "so that their freedom would become the
freedom of God."[45] In this I can do no more than bring to them
the same message the Church has always brought, and yet I desire
to put the old message in new words ... words that ring true, words
so burning and appealing that they sense a new understanding and
appreciation of it, and so come to be born and borne as never
before. Would that my words be original, yes, originating from
the Origin and sounding from my lips of flesh.

Then my eyes may..., will sparkle with the truth of my words, yes,
Your words; and my very bodily presence will radiate rays of truth.
May the so-called aura surrounding us as Your reflection be
effective and true to Your all-pervasive light! Meanwhile, I'll let

Your name Jesus adhere to my mouth, hoping I'll first know for myself, and then later impart to others, the blessings of stillness.[46]

Lord I rest in your response: "Puny worm! Trust in having turned your desire to Me. You must know that before you ask I answer you! So be assured of My desire for you and for My retreatants: for you to speak in My name, and for them to hear with desire and learn from Me!"

2. THAT THE EXERCITANTS MAY BE WELL DISPOSED

God yearns jealously for the spirit
that He has made to dwell in us. (Jas 4:5)

"I tell you, whatever you ask for,
believe you're receiving it and indeed have received it,
and it will be yours."
"Oh, yes, Rabbuni, if only we're truly willing to receive it
You'll bestow it upon us gladly and more besides!
So then, Rabbuni, You'll help me this day
to do all the good that I want by myself!
It'll be an assurance for me
that You will do all You want for me in Your goodness
for the simple reason that You've spoken Your word!"

At dawn

Lord, do You envisage the giver of the Exercises as a master? One
of the early directories allows the title, assuming and even
demanding that the person is well trained in the Exercises.

Of course, for You, Lord, the master is the servant and so for Your
least Society, though sadly not for all who are in it. Anyway, if
only we are not offended by it, we could laugh it away as a joke.

Of course, for You it is really a joke, a bit of humour, a joke with
a serious vein made at the expense of us, and hinting at our ready,
silly vanity. If so, how can I translate Your truth and be a master
and servant at the same time? Shall I say, by rendering pleasing
service to the exercitants? Does that, Lord, square with the

charming definition: "the true master is the one who speaks not to the ears but to the heart"?[47] I'd like to be a little master of that sort, after You, Master. Yes, in imitation of You, Master! As Master You taught as one having power or authority and touched so many hearts (Mt 7:29). As one with the conviction of having been taught by You, Ignatius himself would have the director act likewise.[48] May he then intercede with You for me and obtain such similar grace for me that You intend. Then and only then will the exercitants and I realize the core of all spiritual teachings. None but God being the Teacher, it is God who teaches through grace in the depths of the human heart and mind. I wish that the retreatants learn something of this from the transparency of my bearing rather than speaking.

During the day

Dear Jesus, would that the exercitants were at home with the simple and yet profound truth of the Spiritual Exercises as they keep seeking the glow of the often imperceptible, but ever penetrating presence of God! If only they could be inspired by this hidden truth in my dealings with them.

People ask curiously or casually who is giving the Exercises. If only they had more than ordinary or casual curiosity! I wish that the retreatants had a healthy spiritual curiosity. If they had I bet they would hear of the rumour of angels with God. The truth is that You are in charge of the retreat, directing the Spiritual Exercises directly. You in union with Your Father and Your Spirit are the Director of all that we, both retreatants and I, are going to do for a full month. Would you, please, Lord, anoint me right at the beginning with such an unction of faith that knows and acts? Only then can I offer them the basic teaching, reminding them of their innate capacity for the Infinite, their desire for the Spiritual.

Once I came to hear of Your complaint to a little boy that people tell one another stories but never does anyone tell You one. So let me tell You one about Ignatius: the story of his anxiety as he was not getting a sure guidance in the early period of his new life. How he was ready to follow even a little puppy if it was Your will to direct him through that! How surprising it is when we think of Ignatius, the military leader who only knew to lead others.

I know, dear Lord, the exercitants will look to me for direction and guidance as I am a priest and am the one who is to conduct the retreat visibly. I know that conducting the retreat is no more than prescribing the Exercises, as Ignatius says. However, as he makes it clear, I stand in relation to those who make the Exercises as one who gives the Exercises; they and I are in the same level, though doing not the same thing. May they then know You are the Director of the Exercises, the sole Director of the exercitants as well as me giving the Exercises, the external aerobics. You alone have the care and cure of souls, theirs and mine! May I impress this truth on them! May they and I together do the Exercises each in his or her position, led by You, Your Father and Your Spirit!

This is the principle I rely on for the success of the Spiritual Exercises. It is a principle of truth and hope. May we be activated and energized by this principle as we go through the Spiritual Exercises. After all, it is You who in person communicate to the devout exercitants, who inflame them with Your love and praise and dispose them for better service (# 15.3-4). In a sense, whatever may be our conduct during the Exercises all should end well for us at the end of the Exercises. After all, as the Director with infinite expertise You should take into account all our limitations and even failures and bring our experience to a beneficial and satisfying and purposeful and glorious conclusion. There lies the absoluteness of Your action to which we can look forward without being overawed by You or becoming diffident in ourselves ... but learning the ways of fidelity in joy and vigilance.[49]

So, dear Lord, may I experience Your direction in my so-called direction of the exercitants! May I respond to Your dealing with me in my very dealings with them. And may they sense my role as no more than relative and subsidiary to Your directorial right and privilege. I like to recall Your words to this effect: "But you are not to be called rabbi, for you have one teacher, and you are all students" (Mt 23:8). I like to remember too the confession of your forerunner. When people innocently mistook him for You he was quick to acknowledge his true self: he was the one preparing the way for the greater One whose sandal straps he was not worthy to untie (Jn 1:23-27).

Lord, having You and owning You as our ever present Director, may we know to keep step with Your lead and dance to Your mellifluent direction. I pray that we may do so proudly with a great sense of privilege. So may we place everything at Your disposal, holding nothing back, leaving to You and even offering to You our entire will and liberty, not counting and giving but giving without counting, and so giving with all our heart and finding pleasure in so giving, not to say generously but fully, and so becoming an *anima devota* (# 15.3). After all "we are never so much ourselves as when we become 'capable' of (You) God."[50]

But who of us are so much ourselves anytime and so become capable of You? Whatever the retreatants may be now, I can do no more than entrust them to You as I myself entrust my own poor, incapable, if eager, self to You. Leaving them free where they are at, I exercise my faith in You. They are Yours, Yours far more than mine, Yours eternally. To be sure, many of the difficulties I think I am handling Your Holy Spirit can and does handle much better.[51] The greater the difficulty and hopelessness of the retreatants the greater You must emerge and increase and in the same measure I must diminish and even withdraw (# 15.3-6). Despite the close relationship as a human director I must stand off because of the far greater closeness of Yours to the retreatants. I'll then know, thanks to You, to be patient towards them and not to rush more than You but to let them grow over time.

"In the same spirit, My beloved, you must seek to dwell in silence before Me and appreciate My silent speech and discern My advance and response to you!"

At night

Lord, for all my conscious attempt at purifying my intention in relating to my retreatants, You know there is an inclination to find mutual love in my relations with them. Would You not sublimate this human tendency of mine so that I may become an *anam ćara*,[52] a soul friend for them, one to whom people have a sense of belonging and feel drawn to reveal their inmost self with all its secrets and hopes and intimations and intimacies as to a companion or guide. Just as Ignatius proved to be in relation to Faber, Francis and the rest of his first companions?

Thank You, my Lord, for enabling me to communicate to the exercitants that You are *the* Director and so the Exercises can't fail. Lord, in my conversational communication may I have the pleasure of making them sense Your lovableness and firmness so that they may seek at once to appreciate You without mistaking You! May it please You to draw me along with the exercitants, to make a complete offering of myself, of my powers and energies, of my desires and dreams, and even of my failures and weaknesses so that You may be all in all. If You do so, then they and I are sure to find our levels of confidence that will free us and open us to You more and more, and no less to one another. Then we shall be able to enjoy and share mutually the most sweet fruits of what You share with us.

Meanwhile, Lord, following Ignatius' own insistence, I feel urged to ask You that my shortcomings and sins may not stand as an obstacle to whatever You want to achieve in and with the exercitants.[53] In this spirit, Lord, I love to claim Your words for myself and all retreatants:

I speak to thee, and often counsel thee, because thy director cannot speak to thee, for I do not want thee to lack a guide.

And perhaps I do so at his prayers, and thus he leads thee without thy seeing it. Thou wouldst not seek Me, if thou didst not possess Me.

Be not therefore troubled.[54]

And so I've every hope that as the exercitants make the Exercises, the Exercises will make them! Then we'll find to our delight that everything in the garden is lovely.

And every time I see them let my eyes see You, for You are their light and mine; it is only for You that I want to use them.[55] Then, hopefully, I'll receive from You a majestic and meiotic method of moulding them in their search of You to find You in Your inconceivable majesty and realizing You in Your undreamt-of nearness.

3. THAT THE FOUNDATION MAY BE LAID

In the beginning
when God created the heavens and the earth,
the earth was a formless void
and darkness covered the face of the deep,
while the spirit of God swept
over the face of the waters. (Gen 1:1)

Wisdom is a spirit that is friendly to people.
God knows our feelings and thoughts,
and hears our every word. (Wis 1:6, GNB)
When you search for Me, you will find Me;
if you seek Me with all your heart. (Jer 29:13)

"All things have been handed over to Me by My Father;
and you too.
Know this too, My chosen one:
No one knows the Father except the Son
and anyone to whom the Son chooses to reveal Him."
"I feel assured, Rabbuni, of Your help this day
to do by myself all the good that I need to do for the exercitants.
I thank You for such assurance
that You will do all You want for them in Your goodness
for the simple reason of Your promise that is beyond me!"

At dawn

Lord, the retreat is on already for a day and more. I believe You have "talked" to me and also to those whom I have talked to as a group. Now it is their turn to speak to me in some way about

27

themselves, about their quiet prayer, about their choice actions ... following a practice cutting across many religious traditions – that of the "Spiritual Master"! Will they all come to me, Jesus, disposed to sharing with me? Will they all be eager and inclined to enter into spiritual conversation? Even if interiorly inclined will they be capable of it? What I want to ask You as a favour for my work of accompanying them is this. Let me know how to facilitate their spiritual dialogue, and reciprocate and respond to it, as I myself am a hesitant interlocutor. As they express themselves to me, freely or fumblingly, let me know to interpret rightly their experiences, reactions, movements, hesitations, etc. May this dialogue turn to and become "a gradual formation in docility to the Spirit, through a freedom that seeks to open itself to grace."[56]

Besides this individual dialogue I'll have to engage them in common too, and talk to them. How shall I broach the Foundation to them, Lord? It would be the best thing to propose it in such a way that *the exercitants may have an opportunity of finding what they seek!*[57] I don't know their need, disposition, character, history, etc. But all that is plain to You. Further, You are not indifferent to them but all concerned about them. As You thus read the minds and hearts of us all, would You not put the opportune words in my heart and on my lips ... and into their ears and hearts?

Their Christianity will then be no external reality but something stemming from the heart. Then there'll be an awakening of the spiritual sense. And the spiritual quest that seemed a matter of reason and will power, will sense the power of primal energies and be sensitized by them. My role as the initiator will be to serve as a mirror in which the exercitants will see their own potential and perceive their own personal spiritual future. "The fire may catch after a word, a glance or a touch. It may even occur in a dream. For (me) the initiator, this is a moment of simple transparency in which God sees what He has made and declares it very good. For the (retreatants) in question this may be a dramatic event, or a deep and sober one known only by its effects...."[58]

During the day

Blessed be God the Father of our Lord Jesus Christ who has blessed us with new beginnings heralding all the blessings in the Spirit. Each day is one such beginning as it marks the blessings of the day that include our own daily tasks. May it be an image of the graced time of long retreat when Your Son rises in the beginning to shine all through the following days. May He raise us to enjoy the light He sheds on us and lead us to exercise ourselves as He works the marvels of His grace day and night whether we are awake or asleep.

The one word for all the blessings is creation, both in its active and passive sense. Creation indeed was an original, inestimable blessing! Father maternal, in creation You make the creature be, come to be, breathe alive in Your very presence. Inspired so, I pray with Your inspired words:

> You set the earth firm for ever
> You send the light—and it goes,
> You recall it—and trembling it obeys;
> the stars shine joyfully at their set times:
> when You call them, they answer, 'Here we are';
> they gladly shine for You, their creator. (Bar 3:32-35, JB).

How they do so from the moment they were first blessed! From the very first moment of creation all of creation thus was first blessed! Human creation was doubly blessed ... yes, indeed almost infinitely blessed ... For, I believe, in creation You bestowed a share of Your spirit upon us (Ps 104:29), and entrusted us with a creative task ... making us a little less than a god (Ps 8:5).

So, Creator God, may we sense the splendour of our existence as product of Your creative power and energy ... power and energy of creative love. In creation You gave us to ourselves in such a way that we thought we were our own, we were all of our own making and did not know we received at all anything from anyone.

Would we ever know enough to be stunned by the sheer wonder of Your magnanimous giving!

As You rested in Your creation, delighting in every bit of it and, of course, the summit of it in man and woman, so did Adam and Eve after You ... so may we, learning from You, like the enthusiasts of environment ... only more than they!

Above all, Creator Mother, may we rest in You as we never hear so of Adam and Eve. May we know praise in our life, praise of beauty and goodness surrounding us, praise of life and creation, praise of love and progeny. Knowing praise one knows, even becomes like God! Indeed, how is it possible to praise without being like God, "completely forgetful of self and truly free, with an expansive heart, ready to be awed by the unforeseeable blossoming of a rose, an infant's smile, the tenderness of God."[59] Above all, may I know the praise of You, the source of it all. Where shall we find strength to praise You? For You are greater than all Your works (Sir 43:28). Still I want to praise You though I am an atomic particle of Your immense creation, wrapped and clothed in mortality from my infancy, innocent of morality in my adulthood. Abba Father, You Yourself encourage us to delight in Your praise, for You have made us for Yourself and our heart is restless until it rests in You.

May we know reverence too. In other words, may we learn respect in its original meaning, i.e., of attention to meaning in the deep layers of existence of our own selves, other selves and even other non-thinking selves, attention to the meaning behind all meanings, beyond all meanings.

May we know the service of reverence, service that looks to You and so is ennobling, service that is part of true greatness. May we also grasp the service that looks to us too and which is so self-serving and self-preserving, and so very proper and right! Our service then will be the assent to You, to Your creative action in us and finally to our own meaning, worth and existence!

May we know in our human reflective experience this vital logic inscribed in the depth of our hearts, the very logic that makes the whole universe be what it is. May this logic become part of the reasoning of our hearts ennobling its own way of functioning, an effective reasoning beyond mere correct, logical, rational, limited reasoning.

So may we be swayed by one desire, one sole inclination, one soulful ambition: what is—whatever is—more conducive for praise, reverence and service of God in creation and in life.

So may we know the fundamental principle of God's glory in living creation and human's glory in Creator God.

So may we derive the principle of *tantum quantum*, the working principle of using anything only as far as necessary, that is so imbedded in animal life and in the whole of nature, but woefully alien to human society.

So may we circle around the divine centre yielding gladly to its centripetal gravity, maintaining other relative, if necessary, gravities; always to break off, to blaze a trail like a comet at the least intimation of the Centre.

So may we wake up to the preferential principle that should guide our free choices of life, enjoyment and action, and commit us always to love more.

So may we live by the overwhelming supreme principle of what is more conducive to living fully by means of praise, reverence and service.

Is there any other comparable charter of human existence and freedom and love too by which humans can be all in all, while letting God be God, and so appreciating and rejoicing that God is all in all? It is the fulfilment of Your revered teaching: "With all your might love your Maker" (Sir 7:30).

Yes, love too! Because the Principle and Foundation is all about love, the sweet discipline of love. If love can't be thought of except in terms of poetry, then the Principle and Foundation is the very metre of the poetry of love. Who in fact can know anything of praise, reverence and service except the one who is in love and stays so, long enough? So save me, loving Lord, from the caricatured understanding of the Principle and Foundation and lead me to the depths of unsuspected enthusiasm of love, discreetly and shyly hidden in it. May we thus embark "at the port of our pilgrimage, that is in the supreme love of God and the exact observance of the commandments."[60]

"But however evident these principles and conclusions may be to our reason, so great is the disorder of our passions, and the weakness of our wills, that we shall never have the strength to act upon them"[61] apart from Your grace, grace that does not square with the limitation of reason and therefore goes necessarily beyond reason.

When does one understand oneself as meaningful except when one experiences God filling up one's emptiness? Your creative act, Lord, is the first act of that filling; and every moment of growth is another significant moment of Your continued creation. Abba God, being educated in such faith here in time and over time, shall we all not know fully as we are known fully (1 Cor 13:12)? Once I am persuaded of this abiding reality, motherly Abba, I cannot but be living truly, fully spiritually at depth. I can only be engaged in the pervasive practice of constantly responding to an ever-present God, intimately involved in my life, indeed, in every human life. The rock-bed of such rich living is the *Fundamentum* of human response to You by way of wondrous praise, spontaneous reverence and soulful service. As such it is necessarily my existential exigency; at the same time it is a formative process that knits me to You in an ever-enriching relationship. It is—shall I say?—an experience of my becoming what I am! Living in this spirit I hope to be at once fundamentally receptive to You and responsible to myself and thus co-create myself with You.[62] What is more, co-create others too with You! For creation isn't simply of a mythical past but is the concrete world of the here and now: my community and like communities of retreat, prayer, search, work, life!

At night

There is another foundation, as hidden as all foundations buried under the earth. Isn't it the foundation of our selves? The truth of our selves? In particular, the truth of our selves in relation to other selves?

Here again, Lord, You are the Foundation that founds every other foundation! You are the Lord of truth; You are Truth itself! So are all made in truth, Lord? Being of Your making, are we not to grow in the truth that resides in us? This is something that St Ignatius learnt from You and, in turn, handed down to the truth-seekers plainly but bluntly (# 21.1) aiming at what is best called authenticity. Granting, Lord, that none of us, the retreatants or I, are wholly or perfectly authentic persons—otherwise there is no urgency of this retreat—may we able at least to say that we desire and aim at being authentic!

Lord, You know the truth that the exercitants possess or should possess, in order to confront the truth they will encounter here and now, sooner or later, in the Exercises. This capacity for truth is a matter of intellectual honesty (# 18.1-11) but does not stop there. It has far more to do with authenticity, "the convergence and consistency of the whole human being."[63] Such a spirit will enable us to be capable of thinking, judging and acting with the powers of all our being converging on a single point. Here is an encounter with the truth where our human destiny is to be decided.

May the retreatants be filled with such authenticity so completely that it may pervade their whole engagement in the Exercises.

Would that, with Your grace, they would welcome every little word of Your truth, "understand it, explore it, feel it, assimilate it, and carry it out as much as possible".[64]

Lord, lead them and, for their sake, me too, to have this aim of authenticity—the "presupposition" (# 22.1-4)—reflected in our mutual relation. May we be free from any and every misunderstanding between us. And may we grow in conversion of mind and heart in our mutual dealings.

"Receive this blessing, My beloved! As you ask you must know to receive! I grant you to desire ever more eagerly, to seek ever more wisely, to know ever more surely, and to accomplish ever more rightly My will for your glory and happiness! And further know that in your good thoughts I am indeed speaking to you."

4. THAT THEY MAY KNOW
THEY HAVEN'T KNOWN YOU, MY GOD

Seek Me and live. (Amos 5:4)
Who could ever have known Your will,
had You not given Wisdom and sent Your Holy Spirit from above?
Thus have the paths of those on earth been straightened
and people have been taught what pleases You,
and have been saved, by Wisdom. (Wis 9:17-18, NJB)

"I have been found by those who did not seek Me;
I have shown myself to those who did not ask for Me."
"Thank You, Rabbuni, for removing our ignorance today
and so leading us to do by ourselves
all that is necessary at the start of the retreat.
For all our blindness and blocks
can we be mistaken in sensing
the brook of the Spirit babbling within us
'Come with Me to the Father?'"

At dawn

Dear Jesus, may I know and, so lead my retreatants to know, the
living truth of the *Fundamentum*. May we sense in the memorable
Principle and Foundation the real resonances of life; and may we
not miss in its non-biblical parlance the hidden biblical elán vital
of the Word of God.[65] I wish, Lord, that at every stage of my retreat
and life the *Fundamentum* will come alive with new light and
inspiration and power. There are people who are exasperated by
its very mention. I'd like to be one who is anchored by its spirit,
like so many of Your simple saints or holy savants who knew to

35

savour it! As one of those You have taught put it: "Its truth takes on ever greater value with each new experience that I freely accept. I always return to the same starting point, and each time I discover it anew."[66] As a little knowledge is a dangerous thing let us drink deep or taste not the Ignatian hot spring.

"Venture with confidence into My presence. Don't you know by whose image you've been made and honoured, in whose likeness you've been made glorious! Should you hesitate or fear before the Majesty when your very origin gives you ground for confidence?"[67]

So then I venture to ask that, with the retreatants, I may understand with Your understanding, will with Your will, remember with Your memory so that our entire being and doing may be centred, not in us, but in You.[68]

During the day

I hope, dear Jesus, I am praying aright: I wish that the retreatants may come to know they have not known You, my God. I don't mean to belittle the experience of others. It may however appear antithetical to the eager mood of the retreatants. To be sure, each one of them has had his or her own experience of You. But what could be that experience of You measured by the reality of Yourself? As our Saviour we have a measure, a minimal measure, of understanding You; at the same time as our mighty Saviour you are Lord, Son of God, and so Lord God of all Majesty. So I pray that the exercitants may not remain satisfied with whatever experience of You that they may have had and have brought with them. That they may know that they have not known You, I pray, only so that they may know You more, far more than all this long while, as You are not only in Your saving Love but also in Your Divine Majesty.

After all, Your ancient revelation has it that no one has seen God ever (Ex 33:20)! Your new revelation reiterates it (Jn 1:18; 6:46; 1 Jn 4:12). And yet, the same revelation holds that one has seen You, God, in your glorious majesty, One alone, Your one and only Son. What is more, the only Son, dwelling in Your bosom, Father, He has made You known too. I have learnt too that He continues to do so even now, as He Himself said, "No one knows the Father except the Son and those to whom the Son chooses to reveal Him!" (Lk 10:22)

May my exercitants therefore have the holy, unfeigned simplicity of ignorance of mere babes who would be taught by Your Son in the Spirit ... the blessed ignorance of those burning with eagerness who would want to know more and more ... the urgent ignorance of those who would not rest with whatever little they may have known but look for and open up and yearn for more and more, like Moses of old ... like Ruth ... like the Baptist ... like Mary ... like the first exercitant, Ignatius! And like even me! You wouldn't object to the last addition, Lord, would You?

May they and I know You, Living God, Filial God and Depth God, thus more ... not, however, extensively or conceptually or bookishly even from the Bible ... but intensely, simply, directly, personally, spiritually, truly, humbly, divinely, just as You are and as You are pleased to reveal Yourself. So, my Lord God of pure majesty, may we be blessed with the intimate, profound understanding and relish of the truth (# 2.5) that is foremost You in Your magnificent and majestic reality! As the Hindu, godly Gandhiji was blessed so enviably and admirably to think of You as Truth ... though he was not privileged to know the mystery of the Father, Son and Spirit as triune Majesty.

God our Lord, Your reality is simply Divine Majesty. Is there any other title expressive of greater reverence? Would that we had a peep into such a vision in faith or in whatever other way of Your choice, enthralling and so striking us dead only to be alive! Would

37

that we were struck dead by Your unapproachable light! Would that we were slain by the awesome and yet winsome shine of Your threesome Majesty of Oneness!

My Lord and my God, even Your angels are so majestic. Then how much more infinitely so should You be! The seer John seeing one could not but fall down to worship at the feet of the angel only to be told, "You must not do that!... Worship God" (Rev 22:9).

How shall we worship You in Your supreme, holy Majesty that yearns for us? Not unless we go beyond the threshold of knowledge of God and of ourselves. Like Job, for instance, who said: "I know that You can do all things, and that no purpose of Yours can be thwarted.... Therefore I have uttered what I did not understand, things too wonderful for me, which I did not know.... I had heard of You by the hearing of the ear, but now my eye sees You; therefore I despise myself, and repent in dust and ashes" (Job 42:1-6).

So may we worship You in prayer, letting our deep reverence show from the interior to the exterior. May we gain insight into the significance of the act of reverence at the threshold of a prayer time (# 75.1-2). May we make sense of the preparatory prayer that expresses our worship all round, concretely directing all our intentions, actions and operations purely to the praise and service of Your Divine Majesty (# 46.1). "Sanctify our bodies and souls, our thoughts and our intentions, our words and actions, that whatsoever we shall think or speak or do may be by us designed to the glorification of Thy name, and by Thy blessing it may be effective and successful in the work of (You, my) God, according as it can be capable."[69]

On my part, my Lord God, may I know when to stand aside, with due deference to Your Majesty so that You, the Creator, may deal directly with the creature and so communicate Yourself to the devout soul in quest of Your divine will, and so inflame it with Your love and praise and dispose it for its better service of You (# 15.3-6). Otherwise I should be a fool, a fool's fool!

Finally, Lord God, let me ask you a favour with an Ignatian flavour. It was from the active awareness of Your Divine Majesty granted to Ignatius, that he came to recognize the supreme value of Your holy will and so learnt to be intent not only on finding it for himself but also on helping others to find the same for themselves. May the exercitants and I, therefore, learn the awe of Your Majesty in the discovery of Your holy will for them, which is precisely the goal of the Exercises (## 1.4; 21.1).

Even apart from this Ignatian grace of awesome and yet winsome Majesty, Lord, whatever can we know of You as long as we know not Your will for us? So may we know Your will; may we learn to know it!

Lord God, would You be God at all if You could be fully known to us? Or, on the contrary, if You could not be known at all, say, for instance, in Your will with regard to us, would You be God at all?[70] So may we not fail to know You, as life consists in knowing You.

As the retreatants seek You, I'd also do likewise. I'd seek You in every exercitant-heart that would more or less open up before me. And would You not let me find a little bit of You in each such heart … a little bit relative to Your infinite wholeness? And so I let go my ego and seek to be single-minded in my devotion to You, in my yearning for You.

At night

I recall one celebrated exercitant of old times, Dr Bartholome Torres. He knew theology and taught it for thirty long years. Yet he confessed that he had not really known at all all that as he began to understand and know when making the Exercises! It was his experience that, during the Exercises, what he knew already he came to taste for the first time and be impelled to act on them![71] I wonder if it is not partly because of regular practice of prayer, of being consciously in Your presence, over a long period of time!

Anyway, Lord, will not today's exercitants, far less learned, be blessed likewise with interior enjoyment and exterior flow, yes, even effusion of appropriate, effective action? May they learn from practice that only regular hours of prayer and review will take them into the depths though, perhaps, without their knowing it in the process. May I too have my share of necessary warmth and enlightenment in this regard. Without interior joyous conviction and corresponding action may I become speechless before the exercitants! May they and I, then, receive from You the grace of prayer as You grant us, as You school us in persevering prayer, enabling us to go "a little beyond our comfort zone"; and further the grace of prolonged prayer as programmed by the Exercises to prepare us for Your wonted, if surprising, blessing ... the grace of profound prayer You would programme for us in Your benevolent lead and teaching in examen, meditation and contemplation. Such spiritual respiration of You and me together will illuminate us and lead us in the illuminative way more effectively than hours of study or even deep reflection. If only You would take from me my lukewarm fashion, my lifeless manner of meditation, my dullness in praying to You ... and if only You would give me warmth, delight, life and zest in thinking about You[72] I would be much assured early enough! However, only as You will!

Meanwhile I grow in the conviction that "a man only has the truth to the extent that he acts in truth;" and so "true understanding consists in performing and appropriating to oneself the reality behind these statements"[73] of truth. And so may we grow in our right thinking about You, in our proper affection to You and in our effective response to You. If only we were completely taken with You, taken up with You as the absolute, everything else will fall in place; everything, being relative in comparison with the absolute, will count for almost nothing—*maya* if I may say so.

There are those who not only believe it secretly but proclaim it for all to hear. Like John XXIII who in his opening speech to the Vatican Council had the courage of conviction to declare: "All

40

human beings, whether taken singly or united in society, today have the duty of tending ceaselessly during their lifetime toward the attainment of heavenly things and to use for this purpose only, earthly goods, the employment of which must not prejudice their eternal happiness."[74] Abba Father, may we know this eternal happiness not only in the hereafter but here and now.

5. NOT TO BE MISTAKEN ABOUT THE EXERCITANTS

You live not by your natural inclinations, but by the spirit,
since the Spirit of God has made His home in you.
(Rom 8:9, NJB)

*"I know the ones I have chosen and you too ought to
so that you all may know and believe Me
and understand My accompaniment."
"Rabbuni, Your word goads us on today
to do by ourselves all the good that we ought!
I need no other assurance
that You will do all You want for us in Your goodness
for the simple reason that it is beyond us to justify Your choice!"*

At dawn

Abba, all-seeing, I could in a way hide You from me and so could
the exercitants hide themselves from You. But I can't hide me from
You nor can they do themselves. So we can't be impervious to Your
grace for long.

Given our human immaturity, however, I would ask You now for
Your prevenient grace to prevent hiding among ourselves. Even
if I don't hide me from them the retreatants can hide themselves
from me. This can happen when we fail to understand one another.
There is a simple and sensible note of Ignatian guidance in this
regard (# 22.1-4) to interpret another in a positive light. In the light
of that may we relate to each other with a sense of openness to
one another, truthfully and lovingly. For myself I would like to
act like You, Jesus! When Nathanael mistook You, You did not

42

follow suit but drew him to You by expressing something admirable about him.

During the day

Whatever may have been my thoughts about the retreatants' knowing of You I believe strongly they are known by You. Also You have a way of making it known to them too. So I don't want to be mistaken about their privileged experience. Also I want to beware of imagining and underrating their experience in terms of mine!

It was a pleasant surprise for me to come across an inspired prayer that expressed all that I wish I had with all my spiritual training—a prayer of an American and a soldier, the kind of persons not many, perhaps, would associate with a high degree of spirituality. With him I pray it to You for myself and for those of the retreatants who would need it as much as I, if not more.

> I asked God for strength, that I might achieve;
> I was made weak, that I might learn humbly to obey.
> I asked for health, that I might do greater things;
> I was given infirmity, that I might do better things.
> I asked for riches, that I might be happy;
> I was given poverty, that I might be wise.
> I asked for power, that I might have the praise of men;
> I was given weakness, that I might feel the need of God.
> I asked for all things, that I might enjoy life;
> I was given life, that I might enjoy all things.
> I got nothing that I asked for–but everything I'd hoped for.
> Almost despite myself, my unspoken prayers were answered.
> I am among all men, most richly blessed.

I wish that I was so blessed, Lord God. How can I be so fortunate with little or no melancholy whatever, unless You say such things to me so that my soul can in turn preach to me likewise till I discover the truth of it all soon enough, or at least later if not sooner? Just as was the experience of the blessed, nameless, soldier! Just as was the experience of the celebrated soldier, Inigo Loyola, who had learnt it so convincingly that he could in turn be convincing to others ... including men who did not share his faith and zeal.[75] As St Ignatius intercedes with You for us I pray after him: "May God condescend to give us the grace to know Himself thoroughly and to experience in our soul the presence of His divine Majesty; so that, being made a captive of love and grace, we may get rid of all the creatures of this world."[76] Then I'll need no "melancholy lesson" that human loves have a danger of impeding our relationship with God.[77]

Lord, may I be convinced by You about the real blessedness that comes from You so that my retreatants who will hear me will be convinced too, only all the more than as yet.

At night

Lord, for all Your mystery, You are not far from us. In Your very mystery You reach out to us. Part of the mystery that is You is what You can do for us if only we let You do as You want.

Your servant Ignatius was convinced of it from his own privileged experience. You led him to pass it on to others through the Exercises. And yet he also said: "There are very few persons who realize what God would make of them if they abandoned themselves entirely into His hands and let themselves be formed by grace."[78]

However I hope, Lord, that in Your mysterious ways You would have a way of making us abandon ourselves into Your hands and be altogether surprised by joyous shame and shameless joy. Would that we kept ourselves ever open to You in the faith of Your nearness. Then in the nick of time, Your gracious time, we'll come alive more and more, time and time again! In the meantime knowing my propensity to egocentricity I ask You to permit me not even slightly to get in the way between You and Your retreatants! So "Lord, if You want me to carry on my quest differently than I have done so far, I'm willing to do so, for what is important for me is not the way I seek You but You Yourself. Even if You want me to encounter others differently from what I have done so far, I'm ready to do so, for it is them I want to meet, not my way of meeting them."[79] Then and only then I can be of help to them. So I pray, "Lord, teach me to discover in everyman the unexplored territory which is Yourself."[80] This calls for leaving familiar terrain; does this not, Lord?

If so what do You want me to leave? My natural, human point of view? My misunderstanding? My inexperience? My ignorance? My complacency?

6. THAT WE MAY KNOW
THE MYSTERY THAT IS YOU

The Spirit comes to help us in our weakness.
For the Spirit Himself expresses our plea in a way
that could never be put into words,
and God who knows everything in our hearts
knows perfectly well what He means. (Rom 8:26-27, JB)

*"My dear, the wind blows where it chooses,
and you hear the sound of it,
but you do not know where it comes from or where it goes.
So it is, you must know, with everyone who is born of the Spirit."
"Rabbuni, as each one of us is a riddle,
we need Your guidance constantly
to appreciate whatever makes for mutual understanding.
Such guidance will be no small persuasion for me
that You will do all You want for us in Your goodness
for the mysterious reason that it is within us and beyond us!"*

At dawn

Seeing myself and the exercitants for whatever we are I'm stunned
sometimes to see that we are "beings who are made for more than
we can say".[81] Yes, each human being is destined for God!
However, it is true that we are not always consistent in working
towards our destiny! Anyway, I am coming to see more and more
clearly what happens on the way to this destiny: "No expedition
demands harder sacrifices than does the search for God; in this
search one is continually faced with the total mystery."[82]

46

Caught up in my exercise of inconsistency, fragility and contingence, thoughts flow into me meditatively: "Completely dependent on Him; in my cohesiveness, in my action – in my very perception of Him and passion for Him... The total, limitless dependence: to "founder in it", so that one may expand one's being in *abandonment*, and strive in an effort of *purity* and *fidelity*...." With such sentiments of Teilhard I join him in praying:

> My God, from whom I depend even in such yearning as I can have for You....
> Maybe it is inevitable, maybe it is well and necessary, that I should feel at every moment as though I can advance no further, never sure of the next step....
> To accept and love the feeling of total inconsistence.
> O Creative Flow, Consolidating, expanding, with all deliberation I dedicate and abandon myself to Your universal and deep-seated influences! O God, my consistence![83]

During the day

Till last night and especially last night before going to sleep I was happy that the exercitants were responding satisfactorily. Very early morning however at one o'clock or so, Veena took ill and had to be taken to the hospital. As I prayed over her, I was sensing my unbelief in my very belief because I could not bring myself to take You as real as the night of disturbance in which we were praying. In other words, in some way I was feeling my faith was no match to the senses as I was not able really to face the challenge of the senses, especially the challenge of rude awakening of pain and disease and death, all realities destructive of life.

And now, after leaving everything in Your hands so that it'll reach a purposeful end because You are the Director of me and of the (two) exercitants, I find myself seeing and facing another aspect of the reality of You. What we would consider good and perfect and successful and even holy, You do not always approve of so simply. In what I considered a smooth, wonderful entry into the retreat of all of us three You break in suddenly like a thief in the night and upset the apparent satisfactory progress of the Exercises. And what You do can never be wrong, though some part of us all, I know, will oftentimes be inclined to think otherwise. So it only means all our conceptions of right, success, holiness, etc., have no inherent validity even if we can never find anything of evil in it. It only means that, in the futility of our successes, in the emptiness of our creation, in the nakedness of our being, we should look to You alone in Your perfection, Your light, Your transcendence, Your majesty, Your mystery...

So it is in this way You are bringing us back to the Principle and Foundation, as we stand naked before You, with the mind in the heart.[84] Ultimately (or is it in the last resort?) when we take seriously that the one thing that is necessary is what is more conducive to our final end, we are faced with the fact that there is actually no such entity or experience except God Himself or Herself in the simplicity of pure existence unadulterated by any human characterization or conception even of what we know of love. Lord of awesome majesty, we surrender to You in the mystery of sheer apophatism what lies beyond the threshold of our little knowledge about You and even about ourselves. Such approach to You as the absolute makes every other thing valued aright, not overvalued or undervalued, but as it really is: of little or, of course, merely relative value; and it will hopefully unveil something of Your diaphanous nature. The infinitely great meeting the infinitely small! Can I really relish the great without renouncing the small that I'm used to? For that matter, can I really stay with the small without staying away from the great? God forbid! Rather, let me so renounce the good that is not You so that I may come to enjoy it with freedom and without fear![85]

Lord Jesus, as the Word of God You were with God, *pros ton Theon*, turned toward God, moving towards God. You let it be known to us in Your life as a man! And You want to draw us in the same movement toward God[86] who dwells in inaccessible Light (1 Tm 6:16). And so from the moment we see the light of day we are destined for enlightenment. Our true life which is necessarily toward God grows in taking small or giant steps towards illumination as You keep drawing us! In Your light let us see light (Ps 36:9) and become beautiful, twinkling lights.

Even if we should think or imagine we are shards! Therefore, we pray with the knowledgeable Blessed Newman: "I will trust You, whatever I am, I can never be thrown away. If I am in sickness, my sickness may serve You, in perplexity, my perplexity may serve You. If I am in sorrow, my sorrow may serve You. You do nothing in vain. You know what You are about. You may take away my friends. You may throw me among strangers. You may make me feel desolate, make my spirits sink, hide my future from me. Still, You know what You are about."[87]

At night

As we pray may we know that we pray as You would have us pray... may we have the assurance that we pray as You move us to pray. We could be locating our prayer in ideas, supposedly bright, or else in gut feelings, apparently fervent but very superficial and sometimes even self-indulging. If so, how far we are from locating our prayer in the heart![88] I learnt this myself from those simple souls whom You have taught and also from those tossed souls whom You are still to teach.

> Indeed You love truth in the heart;
> then in the secret of my heart teach me wisdom (Ps 51:8, Grail).

Lord, Holy Spirit, timid and fearful as I am, I believe You are leading me in spite of my fearfulness. And so You make me and the likes of me as God's children ... enabling us to cry out to God, "Abba Father!" In this way, You, are You not leading me, as also all Your children?

7. THAT THEY MAY KNOW
THE DARK MYSTERY OF SIN

Your immortal Spirit is in every one of them,
and so You gently correct those who sin against You.
You remind them of what they are doing, and warn them about it,
so that they may abandon their evil ways
and put their trust in You, Lord. (Wis 12:1-2, GNB)
It was not an angel, but the Lord Himself Who saved them....
He had always taken care of them in the past,
but they rebelled against Him
and made His holy Spirit sad.(Is 63:9-10, GNB)

"Whatever do you want, My love?
It is time you know
all things betray thee, who betrayest Me."
"Rabbuni, won't You, then, shine on us today
to sense whatever we really miss?
As we pour all our energy into the longing of our being
won't You make us make the necessary resolve all by ourselves?
It'll be a confirmation for me
that You will do all You want for us in Your goodness
not to deceive ourselves!"

At dawn

Lord, does everyone find You, everyone who prays? One can call
You, "Lord, Lord," and yet be found to be an ally of the evil one.
Evil abounds everywhere and surrounds us and astounds everyone.
There is no one who does not cry foul! Of course, while doing so,
one is shocked only at another's doing! For all our evil, with all
our evil hidden to us, perhaps, but often enough also plainly visible
to us, we suspect and descry evil around us. But One alone knows

50

and sees real evil—it is none of us but You and You alone. Only God speaks of sin just as only "God rightly speaks of God".[89] May we receive, then, from You the sight to see evil as it is, just as You see it.

I've heard it said, evil "in its pure state" is the "proto-sin,"[90] the sin of the angels, the sin of the good that had gone awry. But of course evil can't be in its pure state but is actually in its most impure state! Lord, I wonder, if this is not a typical example of how evil has polluted all that has been given to humanity ... and so of how the very word world came to signify evil in the bible! Such dark complexion of the world is part of the dark mystery of sin. And yet, good Lord, You see my soul as Your "excellent image and distinguished likeness"[91] ... though I fail and dare not follow suit.

During the day

Michael? Who-is-like-God? Glory be to You, Lord God for Your creation of Michael, of him who is named Who-is-like-God? Michael by his existence is at once the double proclamation of who is like God and who is unlike God. Positively he points to the majesty of God; and negatively he points to the degradation of the devil in its depth of darkness, indeed, to the lese-majesty in his abyss of godlessness. Would that I plumbed the latter to enter further into the threshold of the former. The reason is that though I am not godless I am far from godly, indeed quite certainly ungodly.

The sin of the angels is a revolt, a rebellion against their Creator; against You and none other than You, my God; it is a refusal to use the gift of freedom for You, the Giver of that freedom; it is turning their back to You, taking a stand against Your existential stand and creation drama; it is not seeing and recognizing reality as it is, it is a living lie, that is radically death-dealing.

If—that is, since—God is Truth in all Its blinding majesty, the devil is the father of lies, darkening all truth. Again, if God is Life, stirring and making life burst in all creation the devil is the destroyer of life, murderer and slayer, from the beginning.

If nothing existed till You, the Creator Lord, made everything, what an aping of creation it is that the falling angels choose to perform. They were blameless in Your ways from the day of their creation till iniquity was found in them in an instant, the instant when they set about their dark destruction coinciding with their arrogation of their existence only to their very abrogation.

It is frightening to think of what freedom can do, what responsibility it involves. The greater the freedom the greater the responsibility. But surely it can't be that the greater freedom is left without the corresponding grace necessary for the exercise of that freedom. So, or but, that only increases the deviation or vitiation involved in the misuse of that God-given freedom.

Even human sin at the origins of humanity is no less frightening with its variety of abuse of freedom. We who can seek, O Lord, alleviating circumstances of the gravity of sin can't but be struck by the revelation of the original sin as a free choice of distrust of Your continuous creative providence. Why suspect You of jealously withholding something from Your original human creation? Who can teach us this, except You, unsuspecting Lord? I'm sure of failing miserably in teaching, by myself, this divine truth to my exercitants. May we be open to Your teaching in this matter, as the Elohistic author (Gen 3).... It must have been in a moment of inspiration from You that Pascal realized the human folly of playing God thinking of this or that as good or bad and accordingly rejoicing or mourning excessively at the turn of events.[92] That is what the primordial parents enacted first; and the human progeny has repeated age after age, in person after person all over the earth (Rom 5:12).

Lord, we wait for our own inspiration from You so that we may come to a realization of what sin is and put an end to the old, pathetic, repetitive, self-destructive play.

Lord, I recall here a dream story. You like all stories while I like profound stories such as this one, which I must confess is part of my vanity. Anyhow, I wonder if it doesn't have much relevance here. 'I saw a woman sleeping. In her sleep she dreamt that Life stood before her, and held in each hand a gift – in the one Love, and in the other Freedom. And she said to the woman, "Choose." And the woman waited long: and she said, "Freedom!" And Life said, "Thou hast well chosen. If thou hadst said, "Love," I would have given thee what thou didst ask for; and I would have gone from thee, and returned to thee no more. Now, the day will come when I shall return. In that day I shall bear both gifts in one hand." I heard the woman laugh in her sleep.'[93]

Lord God, even my abused, yes abased, freedom can be disabused by Your intervention so that it will be at the end true, active freedom, bringing with it Life too! Is it for this that You allowed sin, Lord of all knowing freedom?

Only You, Lord, can lead us to meditate so on the history of sin, turning from an exclusively self-centred consideration of sin. As elsewhere, here too, merely self-centred meditation on sin is part of our unsuspected wickedness; or else, willy-nilly it is a part of disguising our wickedness! That means we are not unaware of our wickedness but dare not see it as it is. So, You warn us of having eyes and yet being blind. And I hear You say to me as You did to others: "The fact that I tell you about it is the sign that I want to heal you from it."[94] So, Lord, it is You who can reveal our wickedness and make us survive it for the better.

At night

Good Lord, I've heard You asking "Where are you?" I don't know but You do, Lord! You know how I've ended up wherever I'm. All-seeing Lord, You surely know what I wanted before and what I really want now! Sin is basically a matter of wanting that turns out surprisingly and shockingly a matter of loathing. Sin starts from wanting and ends in wanting, turning into what is wholly disappointing and disgusting.

Now as I meditate over sin and accompany the retreatants in the same meditation what do I want? And what can they want? Through your servant Ignatius we learn to ask for the grace of shame and confusion and sorrow and tears for our sins. "That sorrow from which tears spring I cannot find, such is my heart's hardness."[95]

One young retreatant, authentic in her own way, said that she felt like laughing when hearing of tears for sins. How am I to tell them what You've indeed told someone or other: "Dost thou wish that it always cost Me the blood of My humanity, without thy shedding tears?"[96] With such people and for my own good I am moved to confess: "Very frequently I do not know what I should want; I do not know what is good for me. I nevertheless request it according to the faith of the Church, knowing that God will let me see what I need, if I am trying to do my best. Through my various attempts, God will let me know what is good for me."[97]

Dear Jesus, this is a restless but searching desire in my being. I trust that, through You, our Abba God will accomplish this within me and all those like me or unlike me!

Thank You, gracious Lord, for granting me a new understanding thanks to Your words scattered here and there (Mt 13:18-23).

"We do not understand sin, because there is nothing to understand. Sin is a denial and rejection of meaning, a turning away from what is good, true and beautiful. Its malice consists precisely in its perverse preference for non-being over being, for non-reality over reality. Sin is the ultimate, absurd human act. We can analyze what leads up to it and predict its consequences, but we can never understand what makes a human will choose to turn away from its proper object. By sin we deny God, (the Son of God, the Spirit of God); in the last analysis we deny ourselves. We twist our nature out of shape.

"Because one cannot understand sin, one may be tempted to doubt its reality. Or call it a relatively harmless mischief... Humiliated by my inability to will sin away, I may try to imagine it away, or rationalize my situation. But denial merely renders its destructive effects invisible to me; this is blindness to danger, not freedom. We make no progress forgetting sin and concentrating on "positive realities"—because progress is a matter of a deeper apprehension of truth. Spiritual growth is hastened considerably by one becoming more aware of the *reality* of sin in our life.

"In some mysterious way we attain a depth of experience of God only by being exposed to our sinfulness, as individuals and members of a sinful race."[98]

So we pray our heart out, crying out in awareness of our sin. Grievously bedaubed with the filth that is sin, we sense that we can only keep sinking further if You were not seeking us, seeking to redeem us. How true it is: "I shall never know God if I do not wrestle with and against evil even at the cost of life itself."[99]

8. THAT WE MAY KNOW AND OWN OUR OWN SINS

The Lord fills me with His spirit and power,
and gives me a sense of justice and the courage
to tell the people of Israel what their sins are. (Micah 3:8, GNB)

"My beloved, if you were to know your sins,
you wouldst lose heart."
"Rabbuni, how much, then, do we need Your light
today and everyday to sense the messy mystery of sin?
I'll be then persuaded enough
that You will do all You want for us in Your goodness
to lead us to salvation that is beyond us!"

At dawn

"Blessed are those who mourn or weep; they shall be comforted!" These are Your words, Jesus, traditionally blessed and yet traditionally missed. I never understood them as today, in the continued context of meditations on sin. We mourn "because of the power and reality of evil, for power is still given to evil because of the wickedness of humans".[100] But You don't leave us at that. You turn our mourning into saving grief: the grief that You produce, the godly grief that releases us from permanent, undying grief: "godly grief produces a repentance that leads to salvation and brings no regret" (2 Cor 7:10). Draw from the hardness of my heart tears of compunction—*Educ de cordis nostri duritia lacrymas compunctionis.*

To arrive at such a saving grace of repentance and sorrow, Abba, I must arrive at the horrible truth of my sins that is often passed over or suppressed! But could I plumb the depths of my bad faith (Jer 17:9)? After all, sin in us seems to exclude and does indeed exclude our ready admission of the true sinfulness of sin.[101] Do I have the courage to be sincere, ruthlessly sincere, in my search for that hidden, horrible truth? How can I stand a brutal confrontation of all the sins I've done ... or could have done if only I had the chance? How can I bear my basic falsity, inured inauthenticity, betraying all that I was made for and destined for and ought to exist for? How can I ... except in the presence of One who is at once like me and unlike me—of You, Jesus ... of You as the man of God ... being at once the Father's younger and elder son with a difference[102]—who shed many tears of grief and showed Your heart of compassion to us ... and who on the cross obtained complete victory over evil and enabled us to shelter in Your compassion and share in that veritable victory.

With those who were inspired to pray I too pray: "But I'll come in, / Before my loss, / Me further toss, / As sure to win / Under His cross."[103]

During the day

Abba, Holy Father, you know my nature which likes being good and cannot brook anything bad. It is part of my nature to insist on occasion that people should own up their sins in the proper public forum, say students in the class, the workers before their paying benefactors, or even, as I remember, retreatants before their directors. Holy Father, may I have the grace to own up my sins not only before You, not only in my private forum, but also in suitable public forum.

Holy Lord God, others' sins I have known and understood; I tend to evaluate them in their seriousness. I have not denied my sins, but I've never considered them more serious than those of some other people who have done violence to my freedom and done me harm. I've spontaneously wondered how the earth has not swallowed some of the sinners—scoundrels I called them—who have come my way intrusively violently! I have not however considered my sins in this light. Your servant Ignatius suggests it (# 60.1-4), as other graced persons too have intuited it for themselves. St Gertrude, for instance. Oh! How I wish I could pray like her, "The greatest miracle for me, Lord, is that the earth continues to support a sinner like me."[104] Wherever could I be when compared to such great souls of high spiritual fervour and flavour?

I begin to see, Lord God of infinite majesty, that sins, whether one or many, are really grave independent of their grave or light matter, for the simple reason that they are against You, slighting the gravity of Your majesty worthy of all honour and glory. In our human dealings we make no such distinctions about the failures in relation to the powers that be. Even acts of forgetfulness or omission or weakness are considered downright seriously, if wrongly, and dealt with accordingly. That we categorize our failures in relation to You differently is really a way of minimizing Your majesty, Your reality, Your existence, Your relationship. Is not my faith a make-believe? Is not my faith something that really downgrades Your existence? Lessening You thus in Your unique status, to use a popular word among us humans, I know less of God, I make God less, as far as I can make it, than what God is; and I become indeed Godless. But You remain serenely God's Self: surely it is a mystery of generosity that You don't let an evil deed destroy the doer.[105]

So, Lord God, may I receive the grace to let You, God, be God when I confess my sin owning it in its attempted, if futile, violence to Your dignity. May I have a new sight for this, my God, Your own sight, Your own vision, Your own sense of perspective, value, truth and reality?

Lord God, if David, once the man after Your own heart, so sinned that he had no way of seeing his obvious sin, how much more am

I in need of Your revelation for my seeing my sin? As You did in David's case, would you please send me, too, Your word? Your interior word, Your unambiguous word that is truth, Your word that reveals without threatening, Your word that convicts, corrects and converts, liberates, and so consoles, Your word that forgives and calls ... yes, calls forth me, the depths of me and Your compassion, and beckons me commandingly, even me, to live to the full ... shedding half-truths and half-measures!

It is "against You, You alone, O Lord, have I sinned; / What is evil in Your sight I've done" (Ps 51:4 Grail). "Yet with a contrite heart and a humble spirit may we be accepted" (Dan 3:16). Such contrition and conversion I can know only if You bring it about in me not only from outside of me but inside of me. Let this prayer be my offering: "Take all iniquity away so that we may have happiness again and offer You words of praise" (Hos 14:3, JB).

Your chosen ones knew this grace destined for all, this grace of conversion so ordinary and yet so extraordinary. No wonder the old Syrian monks acted on this awareness that it was better to be raised to life themselves than to raise others to life! As one of them so raised proclaimed: "He who perceives his sins is higher than he who raises the dead by his prayer."[106] He was not being morbid but mindful in the best sense of the word.[107] Obviously, the reason is that it is the knowing sinner who has the chance to raise himself to life! Lord, may Your retreatants and I have this necessary gift for living. So save us from the morbidity of refusing to own our sin. So waken us to the fluidity and flow and freedom of life.

With the awakened ones, Lord, I yearn to discover my dissembling life and uncover it in Your presence at least. "No matter how I view myself—the places where I live, my relationships, the things I do—I discover in myself the presence or the beginnings of Satan's attitude: greed and self-seeking, even in those actions which seem to me the most generous."[108] Even if all this dissemblance were not seen by others and even if such matters were not forbidden by nature or society, "sin—which makes me the centre—is evil, because it is the refusal to love and to live: the absolutely solitary self."[109]

If only my heart could beat in unison with such flashes of my mind! Then I'd "make haste with my repentance ... and not stay one day from amendment lest I stay too long ... (but) cease without delay to love my own mischief, and abandon without a backward look the unfruitful works of darkness."[110]

The more You make me sense this my lot the more I pray: "Hear me, O God! / A broken heart / Is my best part."[111]

That this prayer may be effective thinking let me add the prayer of a saint who did not take sins lightly: "Now, good gracious Lord, as Thou givest me Thy grace to know them, so give me Thy grace not only in word but in heart also, with very sorrowful contrition to repent them and utterly to forsake them. And forgive me those sins also in which, by my own default, through evil affections and evil custom, my reason is with sensuality so blinded that I cannot discern them for sin. And illumine, good Lord, my heart, and give me Thy grace to know them and to acknowledge them, and forgive me my sins negligently forgotten, and bring them to my mind with grace to confess them."[112]

At night

I've heard You, Lord, say: "If thou knewest thy sins, thou wouldst lose heart."[113] You know whether and how much I understand the import of Your words. However, because You've said such words I believe the malice of my sins and I want to sense the abysmal evil that sin is. If only I could know what I have made of the gift received at baptism! But, Lord, who can detect their errors (Ps 19:12) or peer down their chasms?

If only I could examine myself with a seriously practical intent! To find what would appal me: "a zoo of lusts, a bedlam of ambitions, a nursery of fears, a harem of fondled hatreds,"[114] let alone the herd[115] of appetites and attachments. Raise me above all these; and clear me from hidden legion of faults and assaults within me.

Perhaps there are no hidden faults; we may hide our faults, some of us being very good at it always ... and all of us very good at it sometimes when it just suits us. Why do we do so, all-seeing dear Lord? There must be something that we cannot even suspect. What is really hidden is the cause why we hide them. There is the secret evil. Shall we ever become aware of this most secret evil? Perhaps only little by little as we grow in freedom ... as You enable us to grow so ... to the extent that Your freedom lifts up our fallen freedom. Then we shall have an inkling of the true personal revelation, at once disgusting and yet surprisingly divinizing: disgusting because of our sins and sinful inclinations to self-praise, self-indulgence and self-righteousness at the cost of others' weakness,[116] and yet surprisingly divinizing because You are not disgusted with us! "The depths (of sin) are revealed to me only little by little, to the extent that I can bear to look at them and to the extent that I become myself,"[117] thanks to Your overpowering attraction.

It is then that I can pray to You so simply: "O Lord, Thou knowest everything. Thou knowest me, a sinner, and Thou knowest the love that Thou workest in me."[118] These words are not mine but borrowed; still they are my own sentiments; to that extent have they not been put in my heart by You Yourself?

Such sentiments blending regret, shame and repentance are not denigrating or depressive but uplifting and even perfective, perfecting our personality! Thank You, Lord, for Your "severe mercy wielding the double whip of fear and shame".[119]

61

9. NONSENSE OF SIN
AND SAVING SENSE OF GOD

Do not cast me away from Your presence,
and do not take Your holy spirit from me. (Ps 51:11, Grail)
A new heart I will give you, and a new spirit I will put within you;
and I will remove from your body the heart of stone and
give you a heart of flesh.
I will put My spirit within you,
and make you follow My statutes. (Ezek 36:26-27)
The Paraclete will show the world
how wrong it was, about sin,
about who was in the right,
and about judgement. (Jn 16:8, NJB)

"Know of My desire for you, as I keep waiting for you.
And beware of sin and its deceptive desire for you."
"Please help us, then, Rabbuni, to dare and stare by ourselves
at whatever we've made ourselves be.
Yes, You'll help us in our darkness
to seek the light by ourselves!
I'll then rest assured
that You will sanctify us through and through,
and preserve our whole spirit, soul and body
blameless unto the day of Your coming!"

At dawn

Lord, You search our hearts. The very conversion I am seeking to achieve is nothing but what I want to receive from You, Lord. All that I have tried in other ways have proved futile, especially when I realize that, though I may not have sinned in wanton manner, there are no sins—noticed in others and abhorred by me—which are not in the form of seeds in my own self. As You converted Yourself to our nature may we be converted to Yours, thanks to Your eternal hope for us and in us. That will be a basic and, nonetheless, genuine imitation of You, transparent and genuine Lord.

I pray for this grace with Mary, the solitary boast of our tainted nature. We rely on her, knowing that she stands, always beside her Son, as the antithesis of sin (Gen 3:15) that has been at work from the beginning. As a sure ally of her Son she will obtain for us the awareness of the devil's destructive division all through history in human society and in human heart and in human art and craft. As one who had, thanks to Your ordering, never suffered disorder she prays "to order the world once more around Christ her Son"; she will thus pass on to us "that fine feeling for order modelled round Christ, as well as for even the slightest manifestations of disorder proceeding from the devil."[120]

Dear Jesus, my meditation on sin cannot remain long on sin as such though this is what I tend to do and have known to do ... on a surface level, like perhaps most of us. I have however sought to rise higher attending to Your Person, centring my meditation on You. Continuing to look at sin can be only sickening and blinding and deadening. All that undergoes a change when we look at You, the Crucified Son and Lord! You alone can mediate to us from Abba "the sublime grace of a sensitive awareness of sin and the world,"[121] without being defeated and disgraced. You were more than defeated for our sake so that we may not rationalize sin but realize the false reason for sin and beat back sin to where it belongs—certainly, not me for whom You died.

To succeed in this, maybe, I should swing away from rationalization to refinement of good, knowing souls who seem to enjoy a healthy scrupulosity which makes them recognize sin where there is none[122] (# 348.2).

I like the truth You have taught some so forcefully: "Man is not the one who once in a while makes a mistake and God is not the one who now and then forgives. No, man is a sinner and God is love."[123]

"As you realize let it be done to you, My dear! I rid you of the faults which foul you, I defend you from the sins that beset you; I give you my love—fore-give it so that you are forgiven already before you sin!"

Given this Your assurance, Jesus, I know I can live in goodness all the days of my life! "O glorious God, all sinful fear, all sinful sorrow and pensiveness, all sinful hope, all sinful mirth and gladness take from me. And on the other side, put in me such fear, such sorrow, such heaviness, such comfort, consolation, and gladness as shall be profitable for my soul." Thus with better souls like St Thomas More[124] I would like to learn to pray.

During the day

Lord God, when shall I be finished with sin, the sickness of soul? Isn't it the sole sickness that often tends to be long standing if not terminal? We have prayed over the past of sin and the present of sin; and in this very absence of God You have revealed Your presence. We have plumbed enough to cry out: "Who will deliver me from the body of sin and death?" We have learnt the redeeming cry too, "Thanks be to God through Jesus Christ our Lord" (Rom 7:25). May this be our lasting experience, our own exodus into freedom. Ah! here is the real reason for our boast, confident and consoling boast: "God is greater than our hearts, and He knows everything" (1 Jn 3:20).

Resting in such a faith, is there any chance for becoming faithless? Guard us, I plead with You, from whatever danger there may be of our reliance on Your forgiveness turning ... into any sort of irresponsibility on our part ... into any sort of licentious use of our freedom ... into any sort ignorance of Your becoming sin and shame itself in view of our liberation! So guarded, shan't I be in a position to make the necessary decision and go on to make the binding choice for my life?

Does hell exist? It is significant that we have no doctrine of any particular human presence in hell. But, hell exists, certainly as a definite future possibility, indeed an unfortunate destiny "if my sins actually catch up with their sense or rather their non-sense".[125] The same is the case for all those unmindful of their continued sin. 'I am a sinner who is not yet in hell. But without Christ I'm headed there by reason of a "logical" necessity I have brought upon myself and which I cannot escape.'[126]

It is frightening to think, my God, that my activities of my present existence, when gathered and totalled at the end of my time, can end up, if their evil sinful tendency continues till the end, "locked in a subsisting contradiction which never stops disintegrating (the empire of Satan, hell)."[127] Lord, does human nature in its freedom transcend itself for better or worse, and that infinitely?[128] Should it be so? Should my free positing of myself be magnified by You either as blessedness of union with You or cursedness of separation from You? Who will deliver me from this ambiguous power of freedom ... except You? As You did a monk, bidding him: "Remain steadfast in the very midst of Hell and do not despair."[129]

Would that I allowed the full reality to come into me ... into the innermost part of my flesh-and-spirit being! Here and now! May I know Your presence, Your presence even right in the midst of evil and sin! After all You were made into sin and thrust into despair of a sort. May I also know the utter non-sense of hell, which is the destiny of those who make their home with sin, sin upon sin, sin spreading sin, sin "sine fine" (without end).

Should my heart, for whatever cause, lose its sensitivity of Your eternal love consenting to be made into sin, may You scare me by the fright of hell that is right for sure. Oh, may it be so. That too is included in the gospel in so far as You warn people of the danger of ending up in hell that is prepared not for humans but for the Devil and his angels.... This gospel of fear, right fear, can I preach through tenderness and mercy and truth?

I would not omit this meditation for the exercitants though even in the second generation of Jesuits there were some who would not make mention of hell and sin. But singular Jesuits like St Peter Canisius did not approve of such men who were so fastidious enough to please their audience rather than train their conscience.

But, of course, dear Jesus, finally I don't believe in Hell as I believe in You. The object of faith in Hell is conditional: what could happen if I believed not in You, Your life, Your love, Your power and Your victory! If we think of Hell in terms of fire, no wonder You are a greater fire all consuming.

"Yes, My friend, I am a fire like the Spirit that does indeed devour but does not debase; it burns pleasantly and devastates felicitously; it rages against vices only to produce healing unction in you of love!"[130]

So I know ... I have the conviction as it dawns on me: "(Abba) God is not offended by us except at what we do against our own good."[131]

Our own good is, as I sense more and more, not only personal but social and societal! And so save us from our false freedom that can turn humanity into hell; make us free enough to be accountable for the well-being of society and so become responsible for the redemption of the microcosm and macrocosm of our universe.

"My beloved one, I'm happy you are rising above regret and shame of the past and opening yourself to Me loving in spite of everything. That is real repentance ... a reason for rejoicing in Heaven and ... therefore also on the earth. How else can it be?"

I can never stop learning the paradox of repentance. "It is the mark of a youthful spirit, of joyfulness and of the ability to be transformed"[132] in myself that involves more than myself! There is an element of wonder in repentance: one is always surprised by one's existential conversion to the good. So no wonder that repentance always serves as one of the greatest formative forces in history bringing to birth true humanity.

Repentance, the passionate response of love for having been forgiven much! After all I know that without You I could have sinned worse than the worst sinner; I know too, You've forgiven me more than any public, not to say proverbial, sinner—if I may say so—by the very fact You forgave me in advance by preventing, forestalling my falling more than I've fallen![133]

"My son, I don't want you to think about your sins either in general or particular without calling to mind My love always. You had better season your self-knowledge of sin with the remembrance of My mercy."[134] 'And so, all that I ask of you is to remember Me as loving you. So don't lose sight of My Son at the crib and cross. "Thy conversion is My affair."[135] I can't repeat it too much.'

Even as I am led to repudiate my sins, Abba, by Your gift of repentance am I to see, then, You and only You, along with Your Son and Spirit ... in our sins, mine and even others?[136]

At night

Lord Spirit, I wait for Your exorcism of my mind and heart, freeing me for fully living, rising above the enticements and entanglements of neurosis of sin, pathology of sin.

Dear Jesus, I am low, fallen low, lower than my own set goal and ideal, lower than my own estimation. And yet in my low estate I find You lower still ... someone paying the (un)natural penalty on the cross. Just the opposite of what You once told some: "You are from below, I am from above" (Jn 8:23)! A story of Your mercy and madness.

Though You are from above I dare to turn to You because You have descended so low. But being so low still Your real nature of being above shows itself. Even so, I feel drawn to look at You ... to look to You ... because through Your low, lowly presence I sense a perceptible access beyond my state ... to a saving state ... because You are pleading not for Yourself but for me.

As You intercede with Your Father above, I realize You are not exactly like me low. You have made Yourself low, being however really above. Being however on the earth You are in the middle, above us and below the Father ever absolutely above. Thanks to You may we dare hope to grasp the immediacy of Abba above.

In "the cosmos of the middle"[137] You are not alone; there appears Your Mother too, all compassionate towards those below like me. Thanks to the mediation of her who stands with You in the middle may we have access to You and through You to Abba Father. Perhaps the "above" of the Father emerges overwhelmingly for us not in itself but only in terms of our "below" as redeemed by the "middle" mediation.

Mother Mary, with your own kind of intercession may I come to my senses ... and know enough the measure of my lowliness ... and weigh the gravity of my sinfulness ... so that I may find myself, not stuck and lost below but raised above, accepted and yet ashamed though with shame far from demeaning ... because of the One who does not put to shame anyone.

Mary, my Mother, you are of our level below and yet you are raised far above because of your yes to salvation offered by the Father through the Son. So as you pray to your Son Jesus, echoing our cries of yes from below may our cries of contrition and compunction be heard above whence flows compassion, the cataract of divine compassion, to mingle with my tears, hopeful tears of no wretchedness but sheer grace ... because I am a loved sinner, saved and embraced by You in my repentance or even in my reluctant repentance and struggle to grow! After all, "the dark areas of our experience can be the very places where we discover God most plainly."[138] How happy the hour when Jesus calls us from fears and tears of despondency to joy of Spirit.

> Grant, O God, that remembering Your holiness, we may come into Your presence with penitence and godly fear.
>
> Grant that, remembering Your majesty, we may come into Your presence with reverence and with humility.
>
> Grant that, remembering Your love, we may come into Your presence with the trust and confidence of children who know that they are coming to a Father who, no matter what they have done, will not turn them away. Amen.[139]

10. LEAD THOU ME INTO FREEDOM

The Spirit is God's mark of ownership on you,
a guarantee that the Day will come
when God will set you free. (Eph 4:30, GNB)
Where the Spirit of the Lord is, there is freedom. (2 Cor 3:17)
The law of the Spirit of life in Christ Jesus
has set you free from the law of sin and of death. (Rom 8:2)
It is not just creation alone which groans; we also groan
within ourselves as we wait for God to make us His children
and set our whole being free. (Rom 8:23)

"Seek the truth; and the truth will make you free."
"Rabbuni, won't You, then, help us always
to do freely whatever makes for our freedom?
It'll be an assurance for me
that You'll in Your goodness truly make us free
by reason of the Holy Spirit,
Who works within us with so exquisite an art,
that the same which are wholly ours
are more fully Hers!"[140]

At dawn

We all exercise our freedom, Lord, though You alone know what
sort of freedom it is. If our freedom is a "mystery of inner
beginning"[141] we ourselves know how we have not used it aright
for right beginnings but harmful and revolting misadventures.
However, You do not withdraw the honour You have endowed upon
us, humans, letting us be and do as we please. And in Your freedom
You (seek to) liberate our freedom from demeaning and
dishonouring itself and so grant us a new freedom, a higher

70

freedom that, with Your saving help, raises us from blind bonds and unsuspected slavery.

Here I have seen things rare and profitable;
Things pleasant, dreadful, things to make me stable
In what I have begun to take in hand;
Then let me think on them, and understand[142]
With grateful love for You, Lord.

"Freedom is what we have—Christ has set us free" (Gal 5:1, GNB) so that we should remain free. How shall we exercise and enjoy this freedom, Lord? Rooted in this faith of freedom we are determined to come into Your presence every day, at every hour of prayer, to be confirmed in Your gift of freedom, ever in need of healing protection, especially in the face of contrary forces. After all, we can never take the spirituality of our natural impulses for granted as the labour of refinement will never cease, given our wounded human nature.

"I am not aware of anything against myself, but I am not thereby acquitted. It is the Lord who judges me" (1 Cor 4:4). May the Lord judge me now so that I may not be found judged by others!

You alone can judge in a saving manner. If I've sinned it is certainly freely, and yet not all that freely! My freedom is not a knowing freedom; it is a freedom of curiosity, if not of ignorance; it is a freedom of not trusting in You, a freedom of self-destruction and shock. Knowing it all, as You only know, save me, liberate me, establish me in Your kind of freedom, in Your kind of knowing, Lord God all free.

Lord, what You said of Judas may well be said of anyone: "Better if one had never been born!" Irrespective of the final end of the sinner, the statement expresses the reality of one's sin as such! Sin—any sin as such in so far as it is sin—starts a process of inner isolation and degradation of the sinner that is shockingly revealed in disease, death and dissolution, and so speeds to its end of what

71

is biblically and so comprehensively known as eternal damnation. If the end is terrible it is because the beginning itself was, if seemingly good, terribly bad and so should serve as a danger signal to the loss of oneself! If Hell is an ultimate and most terrible consequence of voluntary sin there is another before that: namely, the fact that God died voluntarily for sin!

May I then recognize the challenge to living fully Your call to ongoing conversion, and my desire of the same!

"That is no small beginning, My beloved one! It is leaving the sphere of childish, soft freedom of self-will or self-gratification, and entering into that of strong, maturing freedom for the better in tune with your higher nature. You are thus rising above frustrating adolescent co-dependencies and are growing in responsibility relying on Abba who calls you to be like Him and Me ... as the Spirit blows where She wills!"

With gratitude to You, Abba, may I learn to strive constantly for that true freedom where we live according to the spontaneity of the Spirit of Jesus who tells me and the likes of me, "Your sins are forgiven!" Would that I heard it once and for all so that leaving all that inhibits my freedom I may inhabit real freedom, freedom whose name is God, who is the true guarantee of all freedom!

That I may enjoy such freedom, I pray with one who was free enough to die for You and Your truth and Your freedom: "Give me, good Lord, a full faith, a firm hope, and a fervent charity, a love to the good Lord incomparable above the love to myself; and that I love nothing to Thy displeasure, but everything in an order to Thee. The things, good Lord, that I pray for, give me Thy grace to labour for. Amen."[143]

During the day

Thanks be to Christ Jesus our Lord, who has delivered us from the damage and bondage of sin and death, and who will hopefully train me in growing freedom, freedom from half-measures, freedom from unreal loyalties, so that I can reclaim whatever is good and true and noble and divinely willed. "When we identify with (You), Christ crucified, our spiritual life takes on reality and solidity. Strangely, by facing the worst in ourselves we can begin to perceive the glimmer of a hope that is unshakable. Renouncing the appearance of virtue and the illusion of innocence is a great advance. Confessing our sinfulness, without dissimulation or exaggeration, comes as a great relief. Somehow it confers an awareness that from the depths of our being we desire God. We begin to experience such love for God that we take no pleasure in our virtue – and are not surprised by our vice. We seem to move beyond morality into the sphere of a more personal orientation toward God."[144] Thanks be to You, Lord Spirit, for raising me from my sinking, stinking depths to bathe me in Your sea of love!

Lord, Your own liberating words of freedom are: "Very truly, I tell you, everyone who commits sin is a slave to sin.... (But) if the Son makes you free, you will be free indeed" (Jn 8:34-36). Lord, would that You led me into Your open spaces where I could breathe freely and rest freely and work freely and live freely and love freely.

Lord Jesus, with Your incarnation "freedom appears as such, in the sinful world, of course [there is no other world in our experience], but in conformity with the truth of freedom—not as it exists in us, barely emerging from our sins and still subject to concupiscence"[145]—but as it is in You.

Lord, it is good to hear once again Your words of freedom: "If you continue in My word, you are truly My disciples, and you will know the truth, and the truth will make you free" (Jn 8:31-32) ... free to follow You and imitate You responsibly ... not only in gratitude to the sense of freedom from guilt I've received time and again but also in the incipient spontaneity of freedom from bondage to concupiscence You alone would hopefully share with me.

May we open ourselves to this authentic freedom of Yours, this truth of freedom of Yours, showing through in Your evangelical mysteries. Lord, be pleased to open the secret of its logic, so hidden from our eyes, "the poorly trained eyes of scarcely repentant sinners."[146]

Lord Jesus, as You grant me the privilege of contemplating Your mysteries, may I hope that You will bring about a gradual passage of Your truth of freedom with all its thoughts and feelings into my own consciousness and thus begin to exert a negating influence, in opposition to my sins, on my former activity of unfreedom or fallacious freedom or compulsive bondage. If only I shared in Your vitality I'd know Your peculiar, surprising freedom! Lord, could freedom (ensuing in joy) make any sense if Abba did not exist ... if we did not believe in Abba God?

For this to become a reality, Your Incarnation is the very principle governing the fuller unfolding of freedom in our consciousness and so reclaiming for us our original freedom bruised and almost lost in original sin, and continued to be felt likewise acutely especially at times of our greatest sins.[147]

For one thing, Your Freedom (the Word who IS), infinite as it is, still as incarnate, must grow as in our human experience, in accordance with the laws governing every consciousness in this world. Also, as every freedom exists for another freedom, Your freedom, incarnate and so growing and revealing itself little by little, calls forth my own freedom, and makes it grow according to its growing self-revelation. In this way the growth of Your Freedom is simultaneously the growth of my own freedom ... first, by way of acquiring the ideas and inmost dispositions of Your authentic Freedom and, what is more, by way of a certain doing, namely, a deliberate act of response, response of choice that unites me to Yourself, Your own Freedom.[148]

Then I'll be a *mukta* (one who is totally free) after You, *the Mukta*!

This is admirable; but how far is it possible, Lord? "My beloved one, you should know what is impossible for your fallible freedom is possible, indeed more than possible, for God. So you may well call it, if you want, possible impossibility! Learn to make sense of it with the faith I've given you. And you'll know My help where your faith falters and falls short to miss the target."

With Your prompting, then, such is the grace, that I want and don't want to miss during the Second Week.

So I'll learn to act with the force of no external coercion but the sweet murmur from within, the inner push of the Spirit that is averse to goading but ever understanding, drawing, encouraging, sympathizing and demanding, if necessary, within our capability and never ever beyond it.

At night

Whatever grace, impossible grace, I might have earlier asked for, in whatever spirit, now, Lord, I feel asking now a down-to-earth grace that confirms me in Your protective grace. Believing in Your abiding grace, I sense: 'It is important to be contented with the degree of grace given to us today. The imagined "best" is, here as elsewhere, the enemy of the real good.'[149] In the same spirit I cry out: "I have not gone after things too great / nor marvels beyond me" (Ps 130:1, Grail).

And yet I've stumbled upon the immense potential of Christian freedom. It may not pass for a social revolutionary experience and yet the principle of Christian freedom contains the principle of social and political freedom, for within the Christian communion all enjoy equal freedom through one baptism! How can I exercise it and enjoy it, Lord?

After all I am human and nothing human is alien to me, including the sense of being at once free and not free, on account of my hidden sinfulness known not only to me but unsuspecting others! At the same time I begin to see the truth lived by one of Your recent prophets, Brother Roger[150]: "If we let Christ into our lives we lose nothing of what makes life free, beautiful and great." And "I am lost in wonderment at the depths of Your wisdom when You subject my inner life to scrutiny and correction. It is from a slight improvement in my behaviour that I experience Your goodness. It is from the reformation and renovation of the spirit of my mind, that is, of my inner self, that I perceive Your beauty and attractiveness."[151]

In this frame of mind I would like to pray for all in the words of ancient seekers in India: "*asato ma sadgamaya tamaso ma jyotirgamaya mrtyorma amrtam gamaya*. Lead me from the untruth to the truth. Lead me from darkness to light. Lead me from death to immortality."[152]

Lord, You dwell in truth, light and immortality; even Hindus know You as *jivanmukti*, as one who has attained perfect liberation. So, as You promised, may we learn the truth that will set us free.

11. TO BE OF HELP TO CHRIST JESUS IN HIS WORK

The spirit of the Lord God is upon Me,
because the Lord has anointed Me;
he has sent Me to bring good news to the oppressed. (Is 61:1)
I will pour out My spirit on all flesh;
your sons and your daughters shall prophesy,
your old men shall dream dreams,
and your young men shall see visions. (Joel 2:28)
While they were worshiping the Lord... the Holy Spirit said,
"Set apart for Me Barnabas and Saul
for the work to which I have called them." (Acts 13:2)

"If only you knew what God is offering and
who it is asking you ... "
"Such being Your secret succour You, Rabbuni,
will surely help us always
to be grateful for Your redemption at work in us,
and so be willing to assist You as You want?
If it is not what I really want
You'll let me know what I want
and then lead me to what I should deeply want!
It'll be a steady assurance for me
that You'll do all You want for us in Your goodness
for the simple reason You can't do otherwise!"

At dawn

"Eager one, I give you an open ear that you may hear My voice
calling you to high endeavour. I know you feel ashamed of having

been often enough deaf to the appeals I made to you. Not to worry; for you must know now I want to give you—and I give you here and now—the courage it takes to answer, 'Here am I, send me!' With this you ought to have a conviction, even a vision, of winning the whole world for Abba God."

Your words remind me of Your call to Peter, one call after another for the sake of others who need You. "Simon, you must know, Satan has got his wish to sift you all like wheat; but I've prayed for you, Simon, that your faith may not fail, and once you've recovered, you in turn must strengthen your brothers and sisters."

If I had known burning shame of sin You've made me know the burning desire of love, of loving in return as a befriended sinner. So I pray the hallowed prayer of many souls yearning to be at Your beck and call and serve You as yoke-mates. Saved souls know no rest till they become agents of Yours, as part of Your creative and redemptive reality that rules the world. So here is my desire of desires:

> Give me again the joy of Your help;
> with a spirit of fervour sustain me,
> that I may teach transgressors Your ways
> and sinners may return to You (Ps 51:14-15, Grail).

Holy Lord, sinner have I been; sinless Saviour, sinners all of us have been. As such we have been slaves ... for You said, "Everyone who commits sin is a slave to sin" (Jn 8:34) even as we were under the delusion that we were revolving in orbit around our own kingdoms. If only we knew to accept this truth, comforting though uncomfortable! And there is the greater truth: You were made into sin and so a slave of sin, bearing its marks on Your skin, and so rightly or wrongly enough crucified! If You thus became a slave was it to free us from slavery of sin in our personal being and in our very human solidarity? That is not all ... forgiveness and freedom from sin restore us to our original status of dignity or mastery, yes, even of kingship or queendom. Who would have thought You became a slave in order to make us ennobled? And so let me not linger or waver but break free from being circumscribed and seduced in my own illusory kingdom; on the contrary let me now embrace our privilege which is to render service to the divine Majesty through service to You, the incarnate Word, even as it is the angels'. Where our sin disabled our accomplishment Your forgiveness enables us and achieves the good of others too! For, as You clothe us in Your mercy, You want us to clothe others sinful like us, and so through us exercise Your mission towards the lost souls.

"Yes, My beloved, I wish that you give yourselves for the life of the world ... this world of yours in all its broken beauty and shattered vitality!"

I hurry to respond to You, Lord. Yes, when any of Thy own cries out in need or pain, dig in my ear and throw open my heart and stir us to Thy call to serve with Thee and so serve Thee! Loving as You do You'll show Yourself to us as You take our broken lives and mould them anew and make them whole and so rule the world as Abba God dreams for us!

And so, as we begin to contemplate You with a peaceful conscience, may I receive the necessary gift of illumination of mind to comprehend Your mysteries. I want it not just for my satisfaction but for the instruction of my exercitants.[153] After all, any vocation proceeds from the divine You, and reaches humans like me, and progresses in a constant flow between the divine and human. So impelled to share our faith, we shall hopefully grow in discovering every good thing we can do for You and Your reign (Philem 6).

If I am so bold to make such high petitions, I have the wonderful example of the Samaritan woman who, for all her reluctance and resistance in her sinfulness, knew herself more than blessed to bring others to like blessing. Magnanimous Lord, despite mean, manifold sin that clings to me, if I am led to wish and work for such graces for others like me it is only because of Your goodness that has turned us towards Yourself from our mean, sinful selves. The incarnate goodness of Yours on earth is as high as the heavens; and through it You lead us to catch a glimpse of the infinite goodness of the glorious Trinity. O glorious Trinity, as once again You create Your world by redemption, You are pleased to work not only as Trinity of persons but as infinity of persons including even us, making us partakers of the new creative work that is Yours and Yours alone (## 95-98; 145-147). A daring thought to be sure; but what else can the sovereign Trinitarian work mean for us with "loving awe and awed love"?[154]

During the day

Lord, Christ our King, I trust You've led me into the threshold of Your kingdom. May I have the grace to lead others too after You? Or better, let me say thus: lead me to lead others into Your kingdom. I hope in all this I am not presuming or performing a part ... but only being true to Your work! Have You not rescued us from the power of darkness and brought us safe into the kingdom that is Yours (Col 1:13)?

Kingdom! The word kingdom brings before my mind the pathetic picture of the worldly kingdom and authority as they obtain today around the globe. For instance, who is one Kim Jong Il, once a dictator on the communistic throne in North Korea? Called simply "Dear Leader" by North Koreans, they are made to revere him as a hero of mythic proportions; some are specially trained to give their all, even their life, for his wanton tasks assigned to them! Unbelievable but crazily true!

But so is all earthly political authority more or less. The pageant of the so-called regal dignitaries ultimately smacks of using authority and economy for the self-glorification of the few who enjoy power by the 'accident' of birth. People are so inured to such structures that even sincere believers, even outside the royal boundary, may not see anything amiss in such grand and hollow shows. Yes, they are all grand and grandly hollow.

Is there a mean, built-in streak in us that wants to serve someone supposedly great and mighty? A servile syndrome, resulting from the first sin that refused to serve the One—the only One—worthy of all service? I think of the story of how Saul became the first king of Israel because the people wanted one despite Samuel's warning against the evil of monarchy. I recall too the charming legend around Your martyr Christopher[155] in search of *the greater Thou*.[156] Who can be *the greater Thou* than You, my God? It is when we find You we can serve without any loss of our self, but rather with joyous pride and dignity.

Is that why Your Son, Jesus, who was wholly averse to the way of worldly kingdoms, swore to serve You alone and proclaimed Your kingdom, the emergence of Your kind of kingdom, and set about establishing it? In the process You made him a king Yourself, the messianic king anointed for an unsuspected mission and so turning the idea of king or queen upside down (Ps 2, 110).

"So you must realize, My beloved, it would have been useless for Me to come like any king, a king of sorts, in order to shine forth in My kingdom. But, as you must learn, I come appropriately in the glory of My own order."[157]

Lord Christ, our King, to overthrow all such kingly—though really unkingly, ignoble, inhuman, unholy, unnecessary, oppressive— structures of pride ... and so initiate the rule of God Your Father as it was in the beginning (# 95:4)—that is Your aim and ambition, sole mission and work (Jn 17:4, 6). And accordingly in Your typical display of welcome simplicity, utter humility, gracious nobility and glorious divinity You are every inch a King, the King with a difference, indeed the King of the whole universe.

81

Why is it that You share this Your grand, global mission with us? Could it be that we could offer our help? Would that You accepted our help, even if that meant nothing more than a simple, but sincere, dynamic, spiritual desire[158] to be thankful to You for what You have done in our inner self and structure and outer social set-up? Do I get You wrong, Lord, in praying thus? If I am wrong, Lord, then, could it be that You are offering us *in fact* a chance to offer You our help,[159] our generous help, though not all in the same manner or degree? But all generous: if it were not generous what sort of a help could it be?

But generous—is that the proper word here? Can one be generous to You? For it is You who are magnanimous and generous first, offering us the privilege and opportunity of being of help to You.

So we offer You, unworldly but worthy King, our very selves for Your work, Your global work of re-creation, of justification, i.e., of justice making, of universal salvation, of redeeming all existence even as I have experienced in my own. Having had a share in Your salvation how can I refuse to share in the mission of salvation, especially as You invite and call one and all, not only in common, but singly each person? Would that You inflamed this ardour of charity in me and in mine for Your work! If only we on our part gave our heart, our energy, our whole being to You as You lead us in Your work!

Can there be anyone who will not endure Your work that could entail pain? Or, can there be someone who can only endorse Your inviting work, thinking nothing of whatever it may cost? I dare say even political structures, with all their self-serving paraphernalia, won't disown Your work outright. So what matters is that we give ourselves to Your work in Your distinctive, typical manner of proceeding; and further we need to give ourselves to Your person in accordance with the ways of Your Abba God.

And so we yield ourselves to You and Your dynamics of ruling over sin and bringing it to naught in all the ambiguous structures. Seeing You we follow suit, leaving no room to self-love or self-will but learning the very opposite ... But should You, gracious Lord and King, confirm the paths—the trials and travails—of sins "as the avenue whereby Love becomes present in our human world?[160] Perhaps there was no other way to counteract "the messianic expectations of the people of Israel ... perverted by the devil (Jn 8:44) into a belief in the merely worldly, political coming of a triumphant Redeemer."[161] Anyway, some have remembered Your saying: "He who wishes to see Me and attain My kingdom must hold on to Me in sorrow and suffering."[162] As You say so, let it be so, dear Lord. I need to prove myself thus and in no other way.

We don't understand it all. Still we pray, "Lead us into Your kingdom; and what is more, lead us to lead others to Your kingdom." Because we know what You have done for us already, we take up Your yoke of love; and as a proof of it, we take up Your yoke of work too ... like Mary who pondered and surrendered herself to become useful in the kingdom of her Son ... like Ignatius, who committed himself to the same cause being a faithful, though no blind, servant of the Church, the Spouse of Christ.[163] Can one be a merely interior person, as the solitary Onuphrius[164] or Rocamadour[165] of old, without turning and tuning to be a Christopher, an apostle, that is to say, a zealous worker in Your kingdom? And so shielded by faith we stand ready, shod with zeal for shoes, to proclaim Your gospel of peace (Eph 6:15-16). Thus we aim at serving You in souls that are stranded or lost but never left uncared-for; we support them in their struggle so that they survive victoriously; and we accompany them all through in their continued search so that they eventually find their truth, their true self.

Such souls I want to save further—if I may dare say so—so that they will become God's living instruments "making themselves part of the Divine Creativity that (still) rules the world"[166] redemptively. Whoever knows You as the redeemer will not hesitate to share in Your most wonderful adventure, the adventure of redemption in the world. May our grain of faith in Your kingdom know what has already come about so that we can more confidently herald what is yet to come!

At night

Kingly Jesus, what can be lacking to those who seek purely and simply the justice of Your kingdom, and, indeed, the kingdom itself? To those who have no other blessing than the dew of heaven? To those who are undivided in themselves, though perhaps till now we got it all wrong all along? To those who gaze with both eyes only at the privilege of labouring with You here and now, sure of entering into the destined glory after due victory is won? Yes, of course, only when the fullness of time (*chairos*) arrives! And what You offer awaits us who work, or at least want to work, with You!

And so You confer a kingdom on us, as on the apostles, the same kingdom with which You are covenanted with Abba. You make us then Your judges, saving judges, saviours perceiving and proclaiming Your salvation! So we'll act in the consciousness of persons chosen by God and endowed with a charism for this one purpose: to proclaim that God's promises of salvation are fulfilled and also to vindicate God's rights compromised by sin (Lk 22:29-30).[167]

Blessed Michael Pro, you and your co-martyrs had such a buoyant devotion to Christ the King. And so I pray with you: "Take all from me, O Lord! But give me souls./ In health and fortune, honour let me have no part/ Only give wings to the devouring flame/ That zeal and love of Thee have lighted in my heart." A rubric of adventure where one surely wins when losing, where one wins with God when losing before others.

I'm happy to hear Your assurance, Lord, to grant me more than I ask, as Your beloved, if unworthy disciple necessarily struggling in the world scenario: "Institutions, systems, ideologies and all the vain, futile efforts of humanity that go with them are everywhere, and interaction with all of it is unavoidable. But I can give you freedom to overcome any system of power in which you find yourself, be it religious, economic, social, or political. You will grow in the freedom to be inside or outside all kinds of systems and to move freely between them and among them. Together, you and I can be in it and not of it."[168]

If so, Lord, with all your nascent disciples I pray to Abba God for the world of souls that all of them, with their various social structures, may be of You and will hopefully grow in belonging to You, learning the discipleship of presence coupled with the praxis of solidarity!

12. THAT WE MAY CONTEMPLATE

God is spirit,
and those who worship Him must worship in spirit and truth.
(Jn 4:24)
It is we who worship in the Spirit of God
and boast in Christ Jesus and have no confidence in the flesh.
(Phil 3:3)

"Know, My beloved, the mystery of life I am."
"You'll lead us, then, Rabbuni,
to be alive to Your mysteries especially these days?"
"Are you willing, then, My beloved,
to be free from the prejudice that cannot learn,
to be rid of the laziness that will not learn,
and to be blessed
with adventurous minds to think,
and resolute wills to do?"[169]

At dawn

To be an apostle, not of any kind, however glorious or heroic but
in the spirit of Your Kingdom, Lord Jesus, Your Kingdom meant
for all – *lokasangraha*. Together with the retreatants just as they
are, I begin from tomorrow to contemplate the mysteries of Your
life in order to be impregnated with Your spirit and thus, hopefully,
to recognize Your will. The very length of time—*chronos*—offers
a natural setting for this impregnation to take place; then the
chronos of my waiting will become my blessed time (*chairos*),
thanks to Your waiting for my time. And the prolonged time of
the Exercises provides the sacred chance for this by the extended
period of successive contemplations.

86

Dear Jesus, my hope for these days is this: "Through the very act of contemplating, I become one in spirit with the one I contemplate."[170] It is then that I'll be able "to discover the imperative in (Your) life that applies to me alone, and then to make the (necessary) choice to carry it out in my life."[171]

This act of contemplation is Yours in one way, and in another way mine too ... just as to make offerings of great worth You will have to choose me and enable me for it and I will have to accept Your choice and act according to Your enabling me. "That is the impenetrable structure of grace, which consists in disposition on God's part and in a disposing of self on the part of the person who receives the grace."[172]

Lord, may I learn to contemplate as You do, or as You did! To contemplate meant for me for so very long to imagine the scene and exercise my powers of imagination to the details of the scene, of course, with faith being active. But recently, Lord, I learnt that it is far more than that; and I became aware of the deeper currents of contemplative exercise. To contemplate is to let Your grace of faith enlighten my intellect and to let Your grace of love animate my will. I will then be able to be at home with the mystery, with the lower faculties of course serving the higher. All the powers of my imagination must serve the powers of understanding, insight, wonder, etc. Is it a prolonged exercise of going in to faith, and going out from faith to vision, from belief to contemplation?[173]

Part of our faith in Your mystery is this. For one thing, You are the same yesterday, today and for ever. Clearly therefore Your earthly mystery has now become part of Your eternal existence. There should be therefore surprise—and yet no surprise—that Your Person now bears the imprints of the historical events. And so my contemplation of Your historical mysteries is not merely imaginative but existential![174] Putting us in touch with You here and now! Letting us to rejoice in Your humanity as the way to Abba God and so to rest in it, not as an end in itself but as the way to the end that is Abba God.

Another aspect of Your mysteries is that in each one of them each one of us was truly, distinctly present to Your inner gaze while You were living the mysteries of Your life. Further, along with the inner gaze You exercised Your love towards each one of us distinctly! In other words, You relate to us as You related to each one in the historical scene and moment. In each mystery Your gaze took in each one of those present and Your wish reached out to each one concretely. Though we were not there historically You reached out to us in the present time (as indeed You made clear in Your prayer at the Last Meal)! In Your mystery You are present to us and to all humanity. Now in contemplation of the same mystery we become present to You. So when Your mystery is re-presented to us now, its permanent and inexhaustible fecundity is applied to us at present ... according to the very first, original intention You experienced in the first instance.[175] A rare relish (*rasa*) of reality.

In so embracing the mystery of contemplation may we come to know You ... to discover that You are God's will for us. And so, knowing You thus shall we not come to know "what God would have us be and do in those many and large areas of our lives where laws and rules do not offer sufficient guidance"? Then we shall have Your instinct, "a sort of divine instinct that enables us to discern with increasing spontaneity what response is due to God's love for us."[176]

During the day

Lord God, You have all along contemplated humanity in its glory and its fall. Whatever is man that You should keep him in mind? Or what is woman that You should look down from heaven on those born of women to see if any are wise and seek God?

Did You so contemplate the work of Your hands that You came down—had to come down—to be very close to the object of Your contemplation, albeit to work on it again?

And so Mary set her eyes on You; and so did Joseph. Would that I too could, though I am nowhere near them. But ... or so, then, how can I be anywhere near You to be able to contemplate?

I am not near You, I cannot be; and surely I dare not come near You. But still I see even in my essential, unworthy distance that You have come near me, You are indeed near me. You have not kept Your distance, nor kept me at a distance. Though I would hide You from me, there is no way I could hide me from You (Ps 139:7-12). Your mercy so reaches out to our misery surrounding it, and so penetrating it that our eyes can see You, cannot but catch sight of You.

Dear Mother Mary and Abba Joseph, would you please share with me the grace of contemplation that you both had? I hear you say, "Yes and No! For you have your own grace of contemplation given to you. Jesus, the baby King, has been sent to us, to us all, to you too. Yes, at different points of time." Too good to be true, and yet too good not to believe!

Yet, mighty God, as I see You in the arms of Mary or Joseph, Your ancient words ring so loud and clear and true. "For to us a child is born, to us a son is given and the government will be upon His shoulder" (Is 9:6). As You've connected Your human birth with our experience may we learn to do likewise with Yours, starting from birth, through growth, in life and mission till death and beyond. How truly Your Spirit prompts within us Your desire to reproduce Your life within us!

Lord, Infant King, contemplating You I find, that whatever may be humanity, surely the divinity is not tired of humanity, does not shun humanity but remains always warming towards it. You, the Divine Word born of the divine bosom, leaped from heaven, longing to be with those born out of human stock or urge of the flesh! Your Abba loved the world of humans so much that He sent You to us as one of us though with a Jewish face. Your Spirit comes to blow afresh and quickens the womb of humanity … in the young virgin Mary … so that You, God, would have a human mother and call her Amma or Imma! Oh, how blessed humanity is! Oh! How humanity comes to be blessed just like that! Does humanity hold within itself unsuspectingly a spark of divinity? Does humanity enclose within itself unknowingly a presence of the divinity? What no eye has seen, nor ear heard nor the heart of any human conceived God has wrought for us in his Son Jesus, who now speaks by His silences and will continue it for almost His life time, except for His last few years!

Lord Infant Jesus, You are the image of the invisible God, the first-born of all creation. In You we see the fullness of God pleased to dwell, finding its home of welcoming hands and warm hearts and winsome eyes. You, dear Jesus, are "the epitome of God's love of the world and of me in which the incomprehensibility of the pure mystery is implicit and in which man comes to his own fullness."[177]

You have thus come to be our companion … choosing to empty Yourself of Your divine Sonship to become a "son of man" like us retreatants born of flesh and blood. You, who were from all eternity toward-God (*pros ton Theon*) centripetally, put on our frail, centrifugal nature in all its "awayness-from-God". You embraced the human experience of being far from the Father: "far by virtue of the limited extent of human receptivity, with life scattered over a series of mutually exclusive moments; far by subjecting (Yourself) to the slow rhythms of unfolding human development."[178] And, finally, on the cross You could not have been farther from Abba; for all practical purposes You were a public criminal bearing the undeniable marks of sin and condemnation. All this was not the end—as it was to end only with Your cry, "*Eloi, Eloi, lama sabachthani*?"

How sad, and yet strangely happy, are we to see what we see, though we don't see it all and never will! For we have set eyes on Christ the Lord; and our eyes have seen the salvation which You had prepared for all nations to see. And how happy are we to hear what we hear as You, Lord, speak! For who else can speak fittingly of the Lord God but God ... not before time but when the time comes ... changing the dark of night into the light of day?

At night

Dear Mother Mary, you brought us Jesus and so have become the sure means of knowing Him. God gave Him to you and you have given Him to us. He was given to us ... not only to us ... but indeed to all, as on the day of His birth an angel announced to the shepherds. Give us in turn to Him so that we'll be His devotees and devoted followers and earnest ministers to kindle His fire of love all over!

More than that, Mother, I see that the incarnation and nativity of your Son are the decisive events in the initial unfolding of God's Kingdom which involves the task of a decision or "election" – *sankalpa*, and naturally a deep humble love before God in His first and all embracing redemptive work. How much you figure in all this, especially because of your proverbial humility that admits of no shades but only totality and transparency! If we are not equal to the demands of *sankalpa* or choice of life may we attain at least the improbable nobility of being humble!

However, dear Jesus, if I contemplate rightly Your life stories that are really mysteries shall I not come alive with fresh insights of my own in which I communicate my aspirations to You? And so shall I not sense Your demand, indeed every iota of it? Shall I not dispose of it exactly as You propose in and through the cipher language of the Exercises?

Yes, the cipher language of the Exercises so simple, prosaic, repetitive but subtly sublime with leads to the discovery of Heaven on earth, the progress of earth to Heaven ... even in me and through me, thanks to the visibility of God on earth in Jesus. A language

91

that at once fills me with little respect unto the world of mine and at the same time with great respect unto the world of God's making. O Holy Trinity, the Father, the Son, and the Holy Ghost, Glorious God, may I therefore receive henceforth Your grace as You give, so to set and fix firmly my heart upon You. Then You will be all in all, even because of me?

13. DISCERNMENT,
THE WAY OF OUR BLISS

Beloved, do not believe every spirit,
but test the spirits to see whether they are from God.
By this you know the Spirit of God:
every spirit that confesses
that Jesus Christ has come in the flesh is from God,
and every spirit that does not confess Jesus
is not from God. (1 Jn 4:1-3)
If we live by the Spirit,
let us also be guided by the Spirit. (Gal 5:25)

"My beloved, always know of what spirit you are."
"Such being Your wish, Rabbuni, You'll help us from today
in the art and craft of spiritual awareness.
It'll be an assurance for me that we will come
not only to know Your truth with our minds,
but further sense it in our hearts
and so realize it in our lives!"[179]

At dawn

Lord, may I learn from You to read the signs of You, of Your love
and graciousness towards us in Your dealings with us so that we
may follow Your lead and so follow our bliss.

Your dealings with us will include, among other experiences, Your
clear speech or still small voice or enduring attraction or
compelling distraction. May we become attuned to such advances
of Yours as we voice our own acquiescence and respond in silence

or whisper or in appropriate words such as, "Speak, Lord, Your servant is listening;" or "Depart from me, Lord, for I am not holy;" or "Say a word and I'll be healed!" or "I believe, Lord, help my unbelief," or "I don't know where You are leading and so show me the way;" or, of course finally, "To whom shall we go as You have the words of life?" or "Your will and not mine be done!"

"Searching soul, as you speak you will act; won't you? For this I'll teach you ... liberate you from traps, inherited personally or socially or structurally. You'll then enjoy order from inside out as I'll make you obey the order of the reign of Abba God."[180]

Abba God, as You work to produce such a heavenly state may I remain rooted in this simple faith: You want me for Yourself; You are keeping me for a work as yet unknown to me but destined only for me.[181] You created me to do You some definite service. You committed some work to me which You have not committed to another. I have my mission. I will keep waiting till You make it known to me in this life. Meanwhile, I keep trusting that Your will or work is done in me if I do but keep Your commandments.[182] This will certainly save me from confusing my projects with Yours and lead me to a watchful gaze that enables me to penetrate into the intentions of Your love.[183]

During the day

Lord Spirit, the best discernment I have made, alas, is that I have not been able to make any real discernment. This is part of my knowledge of myself which may serve as discernment for beginners.[184] But going further, I must confess, Lord, that I almost shudder when I'm confronted with questions such as: "Do I have the courage to ask God unconditionally what He wants me to do? What are the "natural" reservations that I make in such an offer?"[185] Can it ever happen that I am "unabashedly true to the Spirit moving through my soul?"[186] May I not hope to receive such a grace of the pure of heart? Then I'll know and not hesitate to walk with a vision of You even when it is not clear but clouded. If the Spiritual Exercises are designed to find God's will in our life taking stock of ourselves, with all our ideas, wishes, moods, struggles, etc., then I've all along failed to do any lasting good to my exercitants! Looking back thus is, perhaps, part my pessimism, Lord? Or truism? Or altruism? Or a small, if unseen, step towards optimism, Your redemptive optimism ... answering my "blessed unrest"?

Maybe, asking this question itself opens me to an experiment of discerning ... that will hopefully prove beneficial for the would-be exercitants and me too. Here is, for one thing, Lord, my awareness of my feelings of inadequacy, diffidence and so of fear of my inability ... slowly turning into a sort of "holy fear" recognizing God's primary role of direction. So moving away from dread because of self-doubt about my performance I choose to focus on Yours; then I see my "doubtful dread" gives way to "holy fear" that bids me not to depart but respect, repent and cooperate.[187] In such an outlook I should say I'm happy about it. I feel hopeful that I could still learn discernment and help others to do likewise. Perhaps the less learned one is the more one is helpful to slow learners as I have observed in my student days; I know poor students consult their companions less bright than brighter ones! Anyway, Lord, did not Ignatius set much store on feelings because You taught him so with the spontaneous practice of discernment? Could Newman have become the great convert that he was, without paying heed to his feelings, as You led him?[188] Feelings competing within us test us, prove us, and help us to refine ourselves, and move us to a higher realm.

What You taught Peter Faber, one of the best directors with the approbation of Ignatius himself, I want to learn from You firsthand, in the measure that You choose in Your love.

Why is it, Lord, the work of discerning the activity of the spirits was considered from the beginning the most difficult task of the Spiritual Exercises?[189] Of course, one reason is that we are all so out of touch with what is happening to us in ourselves, both the exercitant and the accompanist like myself. How then can we recognize the finer movements of the spirits in us? Remaining in the status quo one may remain for long without sensing one's feelings (# 6.1-3); but confronted with a higher status of spirit and spiritual living one cannot but be a playground of competing moods and attacks (## 313-336).[190]

There is another reason I begin to sense, all-seeing Lord. The activity of the spirits will occur in us only to the extent that we have learnt to purify our intentions and to aspire to live for what is more conducive in our relationship with You, for what is more perfect, for what is greater for Your glory, for the classical *magis*. As it was in Your case! The devil would have left You untouched if You were living like any other person. But because You were living as the Son of God the devil came bothering You about it. I'm afraid we don't look to the higher level possible for us, and so remain stuck up in our cosy likes and dislikes, and so we fail to qualify for the possibilities of greater attainment of living in the Spirit. And so now all the more reason there is that willingly I (seek to) let the Spirit forge me as She pleases all through the days to come; then I'll shape up spiritually sensitive enough to surrender to You.

Even in our failure to measure up to the standard required for election of life or reformation of life (## 169, 172-174, 179, 184, 189) one thing consoles me, Lord. It is an encouraging instruction handed down to us by You through Ignatius himself: "During the exercises of the Election the exercitant should not direct his attention simply to the movement of the spirits going on within him, but rather to the love of God which both precedes and accompanies all movements of the soul—and ... this by continuing to contemplate the mysteries of the life of Christ."[191] Is this instruction a help to those of us who are aware of their being unequal to the high task of election or reformation? With all the greater fervour, then, we shall find our way traced through and guided by the searching contemplation of the mysteries of Christ's life.[192] So, Lord, may we hope that our contemplation of You with all our compulsions or hesitations and Your contemplation of us in all Your compassion will make up for what is lacking in our capacity to make the election or reformation ... and surprise us in Your goodness so that we find ourselves, in the best of senses, overreaching ourselves and winning in the internal tug of war!

Like the tax-collector, Matthew (# 175.3), who enjoyed an illuminated certainty as to his personal vocation ... without even perhaps knowing to call it so! The name Matthew reminds me, Jesus, of Your remark: "Make yourselves into shrewd money-changers!"[193] By his profession Matthew knew enough in the art of changing money, sifting the true from the false coin. In his new profession of the spirit was he equally knowledgeable and smart? Anyway, Lord, would You instruct me in Your discerning ways? Though these may be sublime and subtle (# 9.4) they are not only for the spiritual élite! So let me not be wanting in discernment, like good money-changers!

Otherwise I'll be just mediocre or, what is worse, I'll be wiser in the affairs of the flesh or world than in those of the spirit and the divine! God forbid! I want to be sane enough, and grow in spirit and spirit-matters.

Also, I want to help others to grow likewise! You saw to it that even the forlorn woman of Sychar could not help discerning herself nor coming to others to lead them to a similar grace. So, Lord, unlike her, let me not be unyielding to Your initiative even at the start!

In this desire, Lord, I'll simply keep doing what I'd been taught in my first long retreat itself without my realizing it perhaps. I'd beg You "to be pleased to move my will and to put into my mind what I ought to do in regard to the matter proposed" (# 180.1) for election or amendment.

Meanwhile, let me abide by You ... seek to abide in You ... I'll keep myself alert at all times. For I can never know in advance when Your Spirit comes and goes ... leaving us time and again to realize what we are like left to our own resources (## 322.3, 330).[194] If I can stand only with Her support then I must know that I am bound to fall when this support is withdrawn. But surely there is every hope that the Spirit will come in Her own good time again sooner or later (Hos 6:2-3). So with all the greater alertness and earnestness I'll wait and keep waiting and hoping. This itself will be sure evidence of the Spirit moving in me, far more potent than any sensible consolation or élan or contrived spiritual euphoria.

"All this, My beloved, you must know is nothing but a search of truth and finding it ... with My guidance ... resulting in liberation of heart and explosive creativity of mind."

Thank You, Lord, if this is not true transformation what is it? And I'm teased by the thought that such experience leads to nothing short of revolution ... reminiscent of what You did in and through Ignatius and the likes of him before and after.

At night

Something funny I've noticed, Lord, about discernment. I am more sure of what You are doing and how You are directing others. So

I am able to help them strangely and surprisingly in their discernment ... but not so in my own case. I am afraid this is the fate of the ordinary run of Ignatian specialists and Jesuit superiors—You know why I say this to You—some of whom fall by the way, while others live in their glass houses, counselling like the friends of Job contrary to Your Spirit of truth and love or, what is worse, advocating in the style of Caiaphas. Be that as it may, save me, Lord, from such danger of betrayal and blindness I am not foreign to!

"Yes, be that as it may, I want to deliver you, My beloved one, from your scruples about others so that you will be free from your own scruples or, better still, to have proper scruples about yourself! And so, I would ask you to find out what you think you are living for. The more you find out in detail the better. Further, I want you to find out what, you think, is keeping you from living fully whatever you want to live for![195] Then you'll find yourself prepared to listen to what I want you to live for!"

I would like to be transparent and pliable enough to register and reflect Your stimulus in me for my own good and others. How shall I yield myself to You so that You would derail me from my one-track mind? I trust You'll train me to be supple enough for Your moulding me in single-mindedness, in purity of heart (ananyā bhakti). Then I'll find myself on the right track—Your track; won't I, Lord? How I wish to discard all that is only of myself, with all my confidence reposed only in You ... so that Your words may abide in me and I may abide in You and so come to receive all that I ask for (Jn 15:7).

Shall I ever reach that level before I can help others with their discernment? For their sake and for Your glory would You not transform and transmute me—and them too—inwardly by a complete change of our mind, as You are the Master of all that is impossible for us. Then I can hope to know Your will—what is good and perfect and pleasing to You (Rom 12:2)—moving and rising from my knowing to Your knowing.

"Meanwhile, My beloved, carry on as I do: carry on being happy with the exercitants who are happy; sorrowing with those who are sorrowing; seeking with those who are seeking; and patient with those who seem stuck, etc. In this way of proceeding you'll lead the truth—yours and theirs—to victory! Go forward then assured all would be well, all would end well."

As Julian of Norwich famously learnt it from You so let me too learn, dear Guide to bliss. I have heard it said publicly, "Follow your bliss". I have also heard, "Beware of following your bliss". The bliss, Lord, how am I to discern between bliss and bliss? "In You is the source of life and in Your light we see light" (Ps 36:9). Lord, did You not Yourself say: "I am the light of the world. Whoever follows Me will never walk in darkness, but will have the light of life"?

14. THAT WE MAY KNOW YOU, LORD JESUS

No one knows the Son except the Father. (Mt 11:27)
Woman, great is your faith!
Let it be done for you as you wish. (Mt 15:28)
No one can say "Jesus is Lord"
except by the Holy Spirit. (1 Cor 12:3)

"I've come into the world as light, the light.
Come to Me and learn from Me."
"Having spoken such words, Rabbuni, You'll help us this day
in our own attempts at knowing You.
And You will so surprise us in Your goodness
for the simple reason
that it is as necessary for us as beyond us!"

At dawn

Wanting to know—that natural desire for knowledge is quite a human quality at its best and also at its worst. That is why, Creator Lord, You gave us the tree of knowledge, not to forbid it outright as is often foolishly thought but to gain it at the right time and in the right way! Having tried to get it by hook or crook, by all means independent of You, we suffer from curiosity or craze to know some crap or other all the time.

Of course, along with or beyond such compulsiveness of wandering or senseless mind we experience also meaningful search: search for meaning and thought, search for beauty and goodness, search for truth and love, search for joy and peace.

Abba God, knowing Your Son Jesus shall we not know all such reality; indeed shall we not know everything? Not of course encyclopaedically but existentially. If only we grow in relationship with Him we shall know what it is to know, also what to know, also how to know. Being with Him we shall seek aright and find. What? What else but the knowing faculty longs for? It is simply truth ... truth that is You Yourself. All I want is to know Christ (Ph 3:10), always knowing that I can never know Christ enough. Such knowing will create its own momentum of hope and love beyond what I can foreknow or forefeel, because it is all Your doing!

Eternal Lord Jesus, to know You is life, life eternal; and so we trust You'll enlighten our minds and touch our hearts during these days to know You better; then shall we receive Your life and so come to have life more abundantly day after day. May God who said, 'Let light shine out of darkness', shine in our hearts to give the light of the knowledge of the glory of God in the face of Jesus Christ (2 Cor 4:6).

During the day

"If only you knew who is looking at you ..." Lord Jesus, that I may know You as You are, present to me here and now! I know You, help me to know You more! Or rather should I say, "Help my poverty of not knowing You enough, help my ignorance of You, help my habit of ignoring You because of my not really knowing You"?

May I know You, as Mary and Joseph did severally ... through Your gracious revelation in nearness; may Your exercitants, too, know You in the same way! Yet as You have put me to serve them in their days with You, may I hope that, with an inner knowing of You through Your growing revelation, I could be a channel of Your revelation for them? A channel far from wonderful and yet so purposefully empty enough to carry Your revealing light and so serving its purpose.

So many knew You in Your lifetime on this earth. Even in Your babyhood Herod and the chief priests and the scribes knew You but to no profit, let alone enjoyment of You. When You begin Your public service, surely Your own kith and kin who certainly knew You as a relation, equally certainly had no real appreciative knowledge of You ... perhaps for no fault of theirs. Also Your own country folks knew You and identified You as the son of the carpenter and the son of Mary and as one whose cousins were in their midst, but they had no knowledge of Your person, Your personality, Your original image. According to what they knew of You, they were cocksure You were mad! As You went more and more public, more and more came to know You; at times even crowds sought You, having heard You speak and seen some of Your spectacular actions. But it is anybody's guess how many knew You aright! In particular, the high-ups in the religious circle, like the Pharisees and priests, not to mention the scribes, thought they knew You. They knew You enough to hate You, to want to catch You unawares, even to dispose of You.

But may I know You enough to want to love You, simply to love You because You are lovable ... You are love made visible.

Pilate too knew You; but his knowledge too was such he was not unwilling to join the ranks of those who were out for Your life.

Compared to all such knowledge of You, how blessed is ignorance of You!

But Lord God, I want no such blessedness; I don't want to be ignorant of You and so happen to be blessed enough not to be cursed. On the contrary I desire to know You personally. According to Your own confidences, no one can know You unless You choose to reveal Yourself to the person (Lk 10:22). So dear Jesus, may I dare ask You and hope that I come to know You thanks to Your personal, knowing self-disclosure? Let it not be said of me that here is a Christian who doesn't know Christ!

Lord Jesus, I recall some other words of Yours regarding Your self-revelation. Have You not said this also? "They who have My commandments and keep them are those who love Me; and those who love Me will be loved by My Father, and I will love them and reveal Myself to them" (Jn 14:21). May we so come to know You, Lord, as You manifest Yourself, unveiling Your hidden presence and closeness.

"Even as you pray thus, you must know you were baptized in My name; as such you have already a privileged knowledge of Me. And you'll have more of it as you sense My advances of revelation. Don't the stars know their Maker? Don't you know *Amma* (Mom) and *Appa* (Dad)? Even the culprit knows the fellow culprit! So, a fortiori you know Me and you'll know Me more and more!"

Jesus, Lord, Your words bring to my mind other reassuring words: "I am the good shepherd. I know My own and My own know Me" (Jn 10:14-15). Doesn't the ox know its owner? Doesn't the ass know its master? (Is 1:3). Whatever I may be, however I may have failed You, am I not Your own, Lord, just because You are You? So, I like to think, Lord, that I too and the retreatants too know You! Oh, may it be so, Lord, as You say so! Yes, Jesus Lord, as You say so!

At night

I can never stop asking You, "Who are You, Lord?" (Acts 9:5). If that is a question of a converted beginner it is no less of the trainee and indeed even of the trained disciple.

Dear Jesus, I am not without any knowledge of You. After all, Your mysteries I know by memory and, to some extent, even by my understanding. But, dear Jesus, there is more of me than memory and understanding, and I yearn for a knowing of You by the more of me, indeed, the whole of me to which, however, I myself am not awakened except at moments of love. Would Your Spirit awaken me to know You thus in and through Your mysteries?

How true it is that life never ceases to make us enter more intimately into the reality of the one we love ... and so never fails to assimilate us to the other through the heart's striving for resemblance. I wish it to be so with my life in relation to You too! Going beyond mere display of fleeting sentiments, will not my knowing You thus in loving faith result in a resemblance, growing resemblance of You ... through the action of Your Abba and Spirit? Such is Your "prodigious presence" as the Word-made-flesh; and it becomes for us more real—I dare say—than even the mutual presence of persons in our perceptible world! It is with this conviction that I hope, with Your retreatants, to enter into Your heart and so share Your attitudes and become one with You— perfectly in the measure You grant us. Outside this sort of resemblance can we really know You, Lord?[196]

The fact that, in the matter of mutual knowing, You have the advantage of me is a consoling thing. For all my not knowing You I feel hopeful about my coming to know You. I want to know You as I am known by You! You know me, so much of me, that You will fructify my desire to know You. "I do not want to become myself except in seeking You, Lord."[197]

"As you seek Me, you'll learn to hear My thoughts, believe Me, in yours!"
"Will it be clear for me? What if I confuse Your voice with another voice? And what if I make mistakes?"
"Of course, you'll; but you'll also begin to better recognize My voice as we continue in our relationship!"
"I don't want to make mistakes."
"Oh, My beloved, mistakes are part of human living; and Papa God works His purpose in them too!"[198]

15. THE SUPREME GOOD
OF KNOWING CHRIST JESUS

Who do people say that the Son of Man is?
But who do you say that I am? (Mt 16:13, 15)
Do you believe because I told you
that I saw you under the fig tree?
You will see greater things than these. (Jn 1:50)
When the Spirit of truth comes,
He will guide you into all the truth. (Jn 16:13)

"No one knows who the Son is except the Father,
or anyone to whom the Son chooses to reveal Himself."
"Won't You, then, Rabbuni, help us this day
in our little knowing of You even as we keep seeking You?
I hope You'll grant us a serendipity of holy beginning
when You will reveal Yourself to us in Your goodness
for the simple reason that it'll be for Your glory!"

At dawn

Lord, make me know Your ways.
Lord, teach me Your paths.
Make me walk in Your truth, and teach me:
for You are God, my saviour (Ps 24:4-5, Grail).

I fondly hope, Abba, this is the time You'll fulfil according to Your pleasure the promise You have perennially made: "Your Teacher will not hide Himself any more, but your eyes shall see your Teacher. And when you turn to the right or when you turn to the left, your ears shall hear a word behind you, saying, 'This is the way; walk in it.'" (Is 30:20-21)

"Remember, My son, the highpoint of My promise when I revealed My only begotten Son to you all, bidding you all to listen to Him!"

Surely, Abba Father, there can be no easier way to receive Your Son who is truth. Let me learn it from Him, grow in it through Him, and stick with it because I yearn for Him or, at least, yearn to yearn for Him. Then I'll enjoy Him enough to share His knowledge with others in the style that You'll impart to me! After all, from knowing You there comes a fragrance that spreads everywhere (2 Cor 4:14).

Dear Jesus, You are our Saviour, like Your Abba, the Redeemer of old. Having saved us by the fragrant offering of Yourself (Eph 5:2), You became indeed Lord of our life, doubly so. We all know and believe that by Your saving work You brought grace right into our midst. Your life bestowed grace upon us once and for all. What is more, Your life also serves as a norm for us; Your life is a living script for our way of life.

So we see You as a new beginning, a holy beginning, the second one after the first that was creation. In the light of Your face, in the truth of Your words, in the power of Your gestures and in the welcome of Your whole bearing we see Your Abba coming into the open and continuing to work even now, right now in our midst![199]

In every contemplation of Your mysteries of life, as we enjoy Your grace may we also be drawn to know Your normative, formative and so even transformative ways. May we come to like Your ways of thinking, wanting and acting in relation to Your Abba and to Your people ... and now to me and to Your retreatants.

I may think I know You, Your ways, Your options, Your preferences. Let not what I know be a block for me to proceed further and discover the unknown You. If only I could forget what I think I know and strain ahead for what I could get to know! So that I could break through my seeming knowing and come to surpass in knowing ... even to the point of gaining You, Jesus (Ph 3:8). Then

You will be illuminative in me and make me illuminative for others.

As You draw me into such meditation of You thus I wish a fire, a burning desire grows in me to know You more than I've known. "While You break the bread of sacred scripture for me, You have come to be known to me in the breaking of bread, and the more I know You, the more I long to know You, no longer in the husk of the letter, but in sensed experience (*in sensu experientiae*)."[200]

During the day

Lord Jesus, having heard Your own call for help in Your mission, I'd like to put myself at Your disposal ... not so much to labour beside You but, first and foremost, know You. Lord, I recall Your words. "This is the work of God, that you believe in Him whom He has sent" (Jn 6:29). Lord, I recall Your action too in the choice of Your co-workers. You appointed them to be with You first and foremost, and only then to be sent out to work for You (Mk 3:14). So, dear Lord, these days we are with You ... just knowing You, realizing how little we know You, and so hopefully coming to know You more in truth just as You are—above our infantile or impoverished image of You!

May we be *so* with You that we know You. Let it not happen that we should be asked by You, "Have I been with you all this time, and you still do not know Me?" (Jn 14:9) As You are with us ... may we be also with You, Lord Jesus.

Even if the exercitants and I should fail to be present to You may we not hope we will come to know You at least somewhat, even as You know us, even as the Father knows You? That was the grace You extended so graciously to simple people like the shepherds, Simeon, Anna and their kind—all mere babes, and also to their opposites like the unsuspecting Saul.

May the area or experience of our misery coincide, as in Saul, with that of Your mercy! He could say as Your co-worker, "Am I not an apostle? Have I not seen Jesus our Lord?" (1 Cor 9:1). Till we too can say the same in our own way, we will stay with You!

I bow my knees before the Abba Father ... that according to the riches of His glory He may grant each one of us to be strengthened with might through His Spirit in the inner self, in the inner person. I lift my hands to Abba that Christ may dwell in our hearts through faith ... that we, being rooted and grounded in love, may have the power to comprehend with all the saints the breadth and the length, and the height and the depth, and to know the love of Christ which surpasses knowledge (Eph 3:14-19). If only I sought Jesus I would certainly find Jesus. So finding of Jesus would lead me to astonishing power of action: action of loving, sharing, relating, communicating, uniting, unifying and so revolutionizing humankind in humanly unforeseeable ways.[201]

Lord, knowing You, I would not like to be overly attracted by anything else; I should want nothing else, no one else, for my happiness! If there were anything that should make me missing something, wanting something—whether it is earned fame, knowledge, superiority, command, travel, etc., etc.—I have certainly not known You. Paul and many a Paul had known You. Dominic and many a Dominic had known You. And Me ... with the double-barrelled name composed of both of them? I like to pray with the words of the Jesuit martyr Thomas Cottam: "O blessed Jesu, make me understand and remember that / whatever we gain, if we lose You, all is lost, and / whatsoever we lose, if we gain You, all is gained."[202] Indeed how I wish I could count everything as loss because of the surpassing worth of knowing Christ Jesus my Lord.

At night

Christ Jesus, You are the Lord of time, of all time. Save me then from the enemy of time, unreal time, time that is not there, time that has passed, time that may or may not come. Master of the now, command me to be here and now. Then I may come to know Your working that is never finished with the past but is ever continued to the present and enlivened in the present! So may we hear Your bidding us, after Your Abba, "If today you hear My voice..."

In the same way, the mysteries of Your life were not finished and dated and consigned to ancient parchments and today's books. They are enduring for anyone who cares and stares inquiringly and earnestly and longingly, though perhaps not all very logically but a little foolishly. Your mysteries reveal and shape the mysteries of human life; though historically past, spiritually and mysteriously they are all of today, *hodie*, for me here and now![203] Perhaps only the *anima* in us—the feminine in us—can see what is in front of the past! After all, we are all feminine in relation to God.[204]

So, moving thus with You totally in the present, I shall not miss You, Lord. I shall receive the grace of Your companionship, friendship and leadership in loving familiarity. That is my fond hope. I can only dream of being drawn or even swept into the Christ-sphere: Your ever widening atmosphere of now.

If I have begun—if not really learnt—to love You so late let it be that, at least now, I love You at last. I wish to hold You fast in love, "busily to labour to love" You. All along "You were within and I was in the external world and sought You there, and in my unlovely state I plunged into those lovely created things which You made. You were with me, and I was not with You. The lovely things kept me far from You, though if they did not have their existence in You, they had no existence at all. You called and cried out loud and shattered my deafness. You were radiant and resplendent, You put to flight my blindness. You were fragrant, and I drew in my breath and now pant after You. I tasted You, and I feel but hunger and thirst for You. You touched me, and I am set on fire to attain the peace which is Yours."[205]

Such knowledge of You, dear Jesus, so intimately received when graciously bestowed on us by You, will hopefully bring along Your gift of light, peace and joy—in one word, Your consolation, pure and simple and yet so varied (# 314). That will be *the* fruit, greater than any other that I can derive from contemplation of You.[206] After all, any concrete resolution or decision that I may make during these days will be dependent on Your consolation; otherwise it will prove to be futile and fruitless. Thus, Lord, be Thou the Lord of my contemplation and consolation.

Abba Father, with the Spirit praying in me, may I hope that You will reveal Your Son in us (Gal 1:16).

16. THAT WE MAY LOVE YOU MORE!

A man ran up and knelt before Him, and asked Him,
"Good Teacher, what must I do to inherit eternal life?"
Jesus, looking at him, loved him. (Mk 10:17, 21)
The fruit of the Spirit is: love, joy, peace, patience, kindness,
generosity, faithfulness, gentleness and self-control. (Gal 5:22-23)

"No one has greater love than Mine."
"So, won't You, Rabbuni, help us this day
in our desire for You so that our love may be like Yours?
It'll be no small assurance for me
that You will do all You want for us in Your love
for the simple reason that loving doesn't come so easily to us!"

At dawn

You know, Lord, better than I how I have been praying to grow in
knowledge of You. I myself know I am more ignorant than
knowledgeable; and, if knowledgeable, I'm insensible; if sensible,
I'm ungenerous; if generous, not for long. So, Lord, with all that
in the background I'm apprehensive that my knowledge could be
notional and become sterile. So I pray as earnestly as I can, with
the urge of Your Spirit, that I may know You really as You are ...
that I may know You progressively more and more in such a way
more knowledge leads to more love, ever increasing love, more
ardent love.[207]

Guard me, Jesus, from loving a little, just a little. In loving so little,
there lies the danger that "one is immediately satisfied with one's
mediocrity" with no thought of advancing. Lord of lifelong love,
enflame my heart and kindle my love so that I may progress

unceasingly in loving, "further and still further, still further again, ever further,"[208] never satisfied with my small measure of love but always searching and striving for more.

While knowledge leads to love, love also leads to knowledge; doesn't it, Lord of love? The greater the love, the greater the knowledge; the deeper the love, the deeper the knowledge! So, may it please You, dear Jesus, that I may first grow and mature in my loving You. You never asked people to love You; but You did say to those who had ears to listen, "If you don't prefer Me to father, mother, etc."[209] I came to learn such a perspective of love in what is most striking in saints. Let me therefore not talk about my loving You but preferring You: let me prefer You in every personal or social situation of competing attraction; let me prefer You equally when it does not cost or when it does. Is there any other way of loving You, Lord of love? Only then shall I be sure that You've placed deep in our hearts the spirit of Your Gospel. "So let us love, dear love, like as we ought. Love is the lesson which the Lord taught us?"[210]

"My Beloved, believe Me your simple longing itself is your voice of prayer. Trust further your aspirations of love are fine; they are My inspirations in you. Here is My foremost inspiration I want to impart: learn to live loved by Me!"

During the day

"Although I am the very least of all the saints, this grace was given to me to bring to the Gentiles the news of the boundless riches of Christ" (Eph 3:8). Lord Jesus, I have no doubt about it; however I don't know the measure of this grace given me; but I know I'm to do the task of helping out Your exercitants in their search for more and more knowledge of You, an increasing knowledge that will lead to increasing love. Given this task (I certainly did not take it upon myself, much less go hunting for it though I consider myself privileged to be engaged in it) I believe, Lord, You are giving me the necessary grace to proclaim Your riches.

113

GOD OF THE EXERCISES

And in Your riches, love has its own splendour. "To know the love of Christ that surpasses knowledge" (Eph 3:19)! Any love has its undeniable charm ... sweetness ... thrill! What then should be the love that is from You? Your divine love reaches out to us where we are; wherever we are it reaches out so anticipatively, so humanly, so humbly, so simply, so quietly, so perseveringly, so unquestioningly, so unobtrusively, so unthreateningly, so calmly, so persuasively, so encouragingly, so invitingly, so far from conditionally, so far from judgmentally.

Oh! how the love of Christ should be compelling us, urging us (2 Cor 5:14) to love Him in return! With tender feelings surely, followed by generous offerings of greater worth (## 97-98), "consenting to an orderliness of life and to a conscription of one's energies and talents",[211] so that my whole life becomes wholesome, fulsome and so wholly Christian.

At night

"Come to Me, all you that are weary and are carrying heavy burdens, and I will give you rest. Take My yoke upon you, and learn from Me; for I am gentle and humble in heart, and you will find rest for your souls. For My yoke is easy, and My burden is light" (Mt 11:28-30). I see this as a new expression of the old commandment of love: to "love the Lord your God with all your heart, etc.," calling forth a genuine sentiment of love directed to You beyond a mere conviction.[212]

"Right, My Beloved, you are beginning to understand that you are mature only to the extent you are mature in love!"

With Your blessing I feel emboldened to ask for Your love's sake: "Eternal God (Father, Son and Spirit), whom to love is fullness of joy, help us daily to love You more, that daily we may come nearer to loving You as You first loved us."[213]

17. THAT WE MAY LOVE YOU MORE AND MORE

I pray that He may grant through His Spirit,
that Christ may dwell in your hearts through faith,
as you are being rooted and grounded in love.
I pray that you may have the power
to know the love of Christ that surpasses knowledge,
so that you may be filled
with all the fullness of God. (Eph 3:16-19)

"Know you not, My loved one, I've loved and longed for you?"
"Yes, Lord, I know; and yet do I? But You know.
So won't You, Rabbuni, kindle this day our love for You
so that our hearts may be burning and flaming for long?"
"Not only long, My beloved, but greatly!
Don't you want your love to be great, and not small,
greater than your earliest love at home,
greater than your dearest love found in a mate,
and far greater than your nearest love of your life?"

At dawn

Lord, I've known stress and strain in the First Week positively or
negatively, rightly or wrongly, wittingly or unwittingly. In the
Second Week of heights or depths and in-betweens of shallows
in which I find myself may I hope to be blessed with Your
consolation as You won't disdain to come down wherever I am!
If the past stress and strain were of my making, during these days
of contemplation may I taste the delicious fruit of Your making.
Peace, quiet and tranquillity! All of course flowing from love,

Yours first and mine too, yes, my own love for You sprung from Yours, from Your ever beckoning, if receding, horizon of love. Will the twofold love not all increase and deepen in me as, with contemplation after contemplation, You draw me to move toward completeness and perfection?[214]

I wish I could tell my retreatants: "I love our Lord Jesus Christ, even if it is with a heart that wishes to love better and more deeply; but I do love Him, and I can't stand the thought of living a life other than His own."[215] "My dear, your sentiments are as true as simple. Your sharing with My retreatants will prove to be a serendipity for them."

Will they and I come to know that we love, that we know to love and that we are in love? And then will not the moment come, thanks to You, sooner or later when we find that our very being becomes being-in-love?[216]

During the day

To love means for us to love more, at least when we are at our best. But in Your sphere, love does not seem to be loving more. Or is it that in Your experience, loving more does not make any sense? Simply loving, always loving—that is You, my God! "God is love" (1 Jn 4:8)! Devout Hindus too know this as You've revealed it to them in their own traditional background! So now I look for no natural or even human gift of love but supernatural gift, the theological virtue of love.[217]

So we humans, inveterate lovers of our own kind, need to learn love, at its source where alone it can mean something and give meaning to everything. For You, love means loving fully. Any other way of loving is no loving at all. Any other way of loving may be good, virtuous, worthwhile, responsible, true to life according to our shibboleths but it is no loving as known at its source. For You, love means loving generously, fully, completely, entirely, totally, radically, etc. For You love means fullness of life. And so anyone who loves not lives not and anyone who lives by the Life cannot die.[218]

God loved the world so much that he gave His only Son to redeem, remake, and so re-create the world of freedom and fairness and fair love, the world even of me in freedom.

In this new world of Your making, beginning with Your initiative of the incarnation, we hear with every breath of Your Son: "Abba!" In this vocative he was emphatically returning love for love. As a quondam friend once said, "You know, there is no God; there is only Abba!" Abba-All-Love —that is the word of Your Word, the call of Your Son, as He exuded the aura of Your love.

Jesus Lord, may I know love, Abba's love; make me know Your love; and so teach me. By heart I know the old *Shema* of love: "Hear, O Israel: The Lord is our God, the Lord alone. You shall love the Lord your God with all your heart, and with all your soul, and with all your might" (Dt 6:4-5); that You Yourself learnt when young. When will it touch the right chord in my soul? I'll then learn it in my heart. May I see You reach out to me in and with Your love, as You did time and again in relation to Martha, Mary and Lazarus, each one of whom knew Your particular love for each one of them. May Your love touch me. I envy the grace of the Samaritan woman or Syro-Phoenician woman who certainly carried Your love within them even after an apparently chance short meeting. Lord Jesus may we, the exercitants and I, know Your teaching, reaching, touching—loving just as You emerge in our contemplations day by day, unfolding in detail Your noble, magnanimous agenda, first glimpsed in the meditation on Your Kingdom that is also the Kingdom of Your Abba and Spirit.

Your loving knows also longing, longing for help ... longing even for company, company of me and my retreatants. Can our company be befitting You, the King, at once noble and humble in love? No, not in so far as what we are but yes in so far as You made Your desire known! Would that I made the right response to Your humble, noble loving and longing—the responsible response. The response of reverence, to start with! Yes, reverence of love. For love is comfortable kneeling, falling on the knees, welcoming every little ounce of love. Next, response of right action for love alone leads to appropriate action defeating difficulties galore and righting wrongs. What then, when there is an outpouring of love?[219] Will it not set off mysterious powers, activating undreamt-of potentialities ... making my response humble necessarily, noble hopefully and loving boldly.

At night

Loving Lord, in loving You let me not shun the canons of love.... Loving means, in a way, sensibly and happily losing one's pride, balance, reason, independence, etc. Loving means finding something delightful and altogether new in life. Loving means being swept away and doing silly things with great satisfaction for something noble, someone delightfully noble. Love means being crazy and delighting in folly for the sake of love, in enjoyment of love, leaving thus a proof of love. I'd love to love You not differently, Lord! I'd love to indulge in folly, holy folly, wholly loving folly "carrying its own legitimization within it".[220] How else can I follow You as Your disciple?

I hope I am praying in the light of 'the *Exercises* (which) are, in the last analysis, a method in the pedagogy of love.... They root out of the human heart carnal and worldly love, thus opening it to the beams of God's love. A demanding love it is, calling forth in us a response of love and of service. Service, which is itself love.... "The zealous service of God our Lord, out of pure love" (# 370.1).'[221] For this to happen may I be configured to You who loves me into ... whom or what you want: someone greater and greater, someone *major*, AMDG? So let me grow in being lovingly attentive, lovingly intelligent, lovingly reasonable, and lovingly responsible.[222]

"Lord God, O Thou, who art the light of the minds that know Thee, the life of the souls that love Thee, and the strength of the wills that serve Thee; help us so to know Thee that we may truly love Thee; so to love Thee that we may fully serve Thee, whom to serve is perfect freedom."[223]

18. TO WALK WITH YOU
FOLLOWING YOU EVER MORE

Whoever follows Me will not walk in darkness,
but will have the light of life. (Jn 8:12)
My sheep hear My voice. I know them, and they follow Me.
I give them eternal life. (Jn 10:27)

"Know you not, My beloved,
I have not called you to follow Me in vain?"
"Yes, Rabbuni. And so You'll help us this day more than I know.
You'll shape our small, sincere efforts in following You
bear much fruit.
So we'll grow joyfully breathing confidence
that we won't be wanting in Your grace
to follow You with spiritual agility and vivacity."

At dawn

They say, Lord, "*Intelligo ut faciam*! I understand in order that I
may act." It seems to be such a sensible adage. If it is applied to
our knowing You how much we should be following You, Lord! If
we are not, Lord, does the fault lie in our not understanding You
aright but awry? Or, perhaps, the truth is that we understand with
our mind well enough according to our level of intelligence but
we do not understand with the beats and reasons of heart! Lord,
we have a mind and a heart that are often divided! You were one
in mind and heart, weren't You, Lord? Whenever Your mouth
spoke Your very heart spoke and so people were touched and
inspired to act; they understood in their mind as well as heart and
felt moved to act unless, of course, they resisted knowingly.

Whatever I know of You may I love! And then I'll walk with You, follow You with the combined power of mind and heart, mutually drawing and raising each other in unison.

Lord, I came across a secret from a humble soul taught by You regarding proper comportment when contemplating a scene of Your life lovingly: "Write in your heart His demeanour and His actions."[224] Though I feel much warmth in this simple piece of advice may I pass it for the present; for I want You to have Your deportment and deeds inscribed in my heart, so that with You, in imitation of You, I can be sure of writing and rewriting and imprinting them. Acting thus in imitation of You may I not hope to be like Your Abba and know Him too, who Himself spoke in the same vein (Lk 9:35). Draw me after You (*Trahe me post te*).

Then I'll know in my life that You, Jesus, are all-sufficient for me. Grant me, Lord, an awareness that one thing is necessary, that You are that *unum necessarium*; and that to live for You and in You is all! In the process shall I not take after the infinite Abba God (Mt 5:48) and so grow in knowledge and love without end? For You are His infinite Light shining upon me, and Your Spirit is His infinite Freedom drawing me to You.

"My beloved, you are thirsty and you have come to Me believing and are with Me. I invite you, therefore, to drink. Out of your heart as a believer shall flow rivers of living water. You'll then love Me and love to keep My commandments. And so you'll know Me as I let you know Me. Knowing My love you shall not hanker for other loves that might shame you! All lesser loves will quite fade and all lower loves wane! As you believe this My wish for you, you would do well to act on this."

Yes, I believe, Lord; as You enable me I'll act. I've known how *Amma* would love to make herself known by her little ones and draw from them an appropriate response. How much more You should be eager to draw the best from us! With this trust, I need to ask You to enlighten my belief in Your active love of me. The more I receive Your objective vision concerning me and my life in the world the more I will enjoy subjective transformation! Yes, once for all and yet ceaselessly!

During the day

Lord Jesus, You ask us to follow You; and so we learn to pray that we may follow You. But I wonder who follows whom as a matter of fact. Is it not true that You really follow us? Strange, but true.

You came to Your own. Where they were You followed them. That is the mystery of Your incarnation as well as of Your evangelization.

In Your human life it seemed but natural to You that You followed the humans. You wanted Peter and followed him where he was at his regular haunt at night. At dawn You found him at his wits' end. You gave him a word, an unsuspected word, that made him not go where he would. "Go away, Lord," he stammered and shouted. Did he mean You should get out of sight? Perhaps he didn't know what he was saying, as is said of him in another story. Did he mean that You should go away from there and lead him away from his familiar haunt so that he might follow You at last, at long last? Following You is real conversion, conversion that keeps to its newfound course.

When Peter became accustomed to follow wherever You betook Yourself, he learnt a couple of lessons on following You.... First, he learnt how You followed Your Abba God in the small hours in God's open spaces of God's hallowed hills before the cares of the day began to follow You. That was no small lesson he learnt right in the beginning of his following You.... Secondly, as You followed Abba God where He was You said also You had to follow where people were. So You found Your way to wherever the towns and villages lay and to whoever wished to see You or hear You or touch You and be blessed with surprise blessing for body and mind. You had gone to Capernaum and followed the way of Peter even to the sea of Galilee; and Peter felt so mighty proud of it; but he didn't know that, however privileged he might have been, You had many other destinations to follow ... not one or two or three, but so many dotting all over the length and breadth of the land: Cana not far from the present day Kfar Nahum, Magdala on the other side of the Sea, Naim, Tabor, Nazareth itself, Bethsaida, Bethany, and above all Jerusalem!

Would that we may know and realize Your warm, if paradoxical, injunction to follow You when in fact You never cease to follow strange places, stranger persons in the strangest of ways.

Lord, we can't certainly follow You unless we see You beckoning us ... or hear You bidding us to follow You. And we can't hear it unless You've followed us where, or even wherever, we are, calmly assured or doubtfully drifting or comfortably cosy or gone astray wittingly or unwittingly only to find ourselves really, uncomfortably naked. How long shall we make You wander in Your following of us before You succeed in making us follow You ... before You make us succeed in following You? Let it not be too very long, Lord!

We'll then seek not only to imitate You, but also to Christify the world, to contribute, in the measure of powers and graces with which God calls me, to the realization of the plan of God who wishes to recapitulate all things in You.[225]

Anyway, Lord, forbid that I ever want to be "a disciple at second hand."[226]

At night

How true it is that "we are shaped and fashioned by what we love"![227] Can I then be sure and proud of my shape and fashion, Lord?

Being familiar with the idea of following You I was made to rethink it when I came across this maverick picture. "A follower is one who is not yet a disciple, attracted but not fallen yet into the trap of the Master. He cannot leave him, but also cannot trust him."[228]

I don't believe You will trap me and I hope I trust You. How much or how little ... all that You know, Master! May I learn to trust You returning Your trust in me, in some slight but sincere way. I'll then imperceptibly mature in my affinity to You, with my hesitations gone. I'll act in growing consistency, having no other mind than Yours and so follow You in truth and loyalty worthy of Your disciples, though indeed never worthy of Your grace ... of following!

May it please Our Lady "to intercede between us sinners and her Son, and to obtain for us in our labours and toil that our weak and sorry hearts may be changed into strong and joyful ones to His praise."[229]

19. WALKING WITH THE SENSES SPIRITUALIZED

Jesus rejoiced in the Holy Spirit and said,
"I thank You, Father, Lord of heaven and earth,
because You have hidden these things
from the wise and the intelligent
and have revealed them to infants." (Lk 10:21)
Take up the whole armour of God:
the belt of truth around your waist,
the breastplate of righteousness,
shoes to proclaim the gospel of peace.
With all of these, take the shield of faith,
to quench all the flaming arrows of the evil one.
Take the helmet of salvation, and the sword of the Spirit,
which is the word of God. (Eph 6:13-17)

"Come, follow Me.
You've heard Me say this before.
You'll hear it time and again."
"May we, then, know joy in ever following You
as You, Rabbuni, thus help us beckoning us again today?
I see it as a marvellous assurance for us
that You will do all You have planned for us in Your goodness
as Your Spirit more and more takes over in our lives!"

At dawn

All is gift from You, Abba God; particularly so are the senses. We use them to touch the world and to take from the world, to be in touch with ourselves and to be in contact with the world, and thus

125

to be and to move about in the world in and out of our selves. So, Papa God, You, who are invisible, become visible and tangible in and through the visibility of Your Son. So we can enter into Your world and dwell in it.

Son of God, You appeared in flesh as the son of Your mother Mary. As such You are the image of the invisible God. However, for us today You are not visible except by way of imagination! Of course our imagination has its own power of lending or creating visibility to the sacred mysteries of Your life. So, while contemplating, even if I succeed in seeing You thus with my imaginative eyes, how can I exercise my other senses? Have I the ability to smell and taste divine things, things that are not of this world? "It all goes to suggest there is an ominous gap between the ideas we form in prayer and the way we ponder them in our hearts. There is a sort of schizophrenia in the vital core of our meditation, and the mysterious contacts between head and heart have been cut off. But all integral human attitudes culminate in our physical senses."[230] Won't You, then, make our prayers too likewise integral to our life and activity? If only my prayer were connected with the whole of my self, and so of my mind and my body!

As I continue with the Exercises, let me learn, Lord, from Your instruction pertaining to the method of application of senses: "Blessed is the soul that hears the Lord speaking within her... Blessed are the ears which receive the sweet murmur of divine inspirations, and which pay no attention to the whispers of this world.... Blessed are the eyes which, closed to external things, are attentive to the interior. Blessed are they who penetrate interior things, and try to prepare themselves more and more by daily exercises, to understand heavenly secrets. Blessed are they who ardently desire to attend to God."[231]

During the day

Lord Jesus, part of my existential structure is the act of following. Following almost defines my existence, my existence as a human being. I wonder, Lord, if ever there is any moment when I don't follow the inclination or attraction that leads me somewhere out of myself, except perhaps in sleep.

To be sure, Lord, during the hours of sleep I am not turned outside but inside, apparently at rest. There are those moments of sleep ... moments of dreams, when in my unconscious I am often enough turned on to myself restlessly, because of my own inner struggles and conflicts, all of which make me only aware of my lack of sufficiency within myself. So, if in dreams I don't exist out of myself, I am only actually made aware of the insufficiency in myself, so that I am urged to seek my sufficiency outside.

In my waking life, my insufficiency is certainly not in the fore. But if I really observe myself and watch my experience of the flowing moments, I can't deny I constantly make an exit! In my restless insufficiency, hardly realized, I constantly flow out to find a level ... a greater level of my existence ... a higher level of my life.

This experience of my unceasing flowing out I see for myself, Lord, in the way my senses follow the hundred and one attractions and stimulants. This sensible gravitation for gratification is the law of gravity of human life, so grooved and grown in the five senses! That I may be full ... that my life may be full of happiness ... my eyes go out looking and seeking and gazing and gaping and grasping. And the other senses follow suit. Each one of them completes the motion set by the roaming eye. Hearing has its antennae all alert to capture waves of pleasure ... smell is all set to smother its target ... taste leaves nothing untouched; touch has its touch buds ever stirring for action! Thus all my senses are so ablaze and alive, often enough if not always.

My Lord, in my contemplation of You may all my senses come alive with a new human sense. Would You not, please, give each one of them a new sense of direction and movement and destination? Make my senses sensible, not as before ... but fully alive with a good sense, a genuinely human sense, inclined to divine sense! May each one of them find its noble, proportionate stimulant not, as usual, in my little scene of life of shadow and shadowy gratification ... but in Your sphere of life, light, sound, smell, taste and touch! May Your contemplative love of me transform my animal nature into spiritual nature, imbuing every inclination, affection and action with Your Spirit. With each sense so spiritualized and wholly moved by Your love, we hope to follow You wherever You go, and serve the cause of Abba God on the planet. Then we will see as You see, hear as You hear, taste as You taste, touch as You touch, smell as You smell.

So, my Lord, let me pray with my five senses ... and let the prayer inspired by Your Spirit glow in them so that we all, my exercitants and I, with unveiled faces, beholding the glory that is Yours, may be changed into Your likeness. Shall I dare add hopefully, even from one degree of glory to another (2 Cor 3:18)?

So, my Jesus, from constancy of faith may I receive the power to hear? From insight into faith may I receive the power of vision? From hope may I receive the power to smell? From union in love may I receive the power to touch? From the enjoyment of love may I receive the power to taste?[232]

Lord, isn't it true that You give these helps of grace to those whom You love? Then I make bold to hope for the same even for those of us who fall short of loving You ... but desire to love You ... love to love You? After all, You are the living Icon made for us by Abba God so that deep within Your humanity something profoundly divine may come to be within our human reach, the reach of our senses! Surely the worship of You, the Word with our human senses, can't but make us bodily alive with delight: touching, tasting, smelling, seeing and hearing ... and thus continuously being with You ... and walking with You! Lord, thanks to You I stumbled upon something precious in this regard: Once we have begun our journey with You we must necessarily continue to walk with You if we are to arrive at our goal.[233]

"My dear, I am happy about your enthusiasm. However, after some time of testing this counsel may sound to you more challenging than comforting. But I assure you it will not be so for long; in fact, before long it will be the other way about. With your interior senses you'll intuit and become alive to My presence. As you perceive Me as the terminal goal far away you'll recognize Me as also the tangible way to the goal, the asymptotic goal. There lies the comforting counsel: I am the visible way to the truth that is life."

Yes, Lord of Life-Way, all this brings me to relish You here and now with the whole of myself, preparing myself for the better yet to come.[234] As we make a point of following You, and rise above the temptation to look behind, we too will discover what St Catherine of Siena learnt from You: "All the way to Heaven is Heaven because You assured us You are the Way!"

At night

Lord, may I learn to appreciate the sensory or even sensuous instructions for prayer and to maximize their usefulness (## 6.2-3; 73-77). The "Composition of Place may seem trivial but it turns everywhere into a symbol of truths which are beyond visualization."[235] It is a re-enacting of what You did first in Your historical rendezvous with Your family and neighbourhood! You composed a place for Your revelation of Yourself to humanity at the start of fullness of time. The same we do today to be present and alive to Your revelation in our ripe time. The more we become present to You inside ourselves the more alive will our senses too come into play, leading to the application of the senses that turns out to be "a simple yet sublime way of making conceivable what is beyond conceiving."[236]

I trust that in Your incarnate ardour You will bring this to pass sooner or later according to Your design ... for me and those that matter to me. Meanwhile I wait for the "hour when, so to speak, the nerves of the soul have been laid bare, so that they are able to react sensitively to the light, the words, the fragrance and the very shape of divine things, in the same way as the nerves of the body, with a spontaneity which does not need to be learnt."[237] In this way I'll live Your kind of life! And You'll live mine and ours! And then I'll live even others' life.[238] Isn't it a wonderful mission, so much like Yours?

Mary our Mother, more than you whoever vibrated with such spontaneity? Your *Magnificat* witnesses to it. You rejoiced and grew to rejoice in your mission of making Jesus known, loved and served. Would you not, please, fulfil your maternal mission in relation to us now, even as you remind us gently and tenderly that we are known, loved and served by the living God.[239] Lead us further more to do whatever He bids us do!

20. ARDUOUS ADVENTURE UNDER CHRIST'S STANDARD

The Spirit drove Him out into the wilderness.
He was in the wilderness forty days, tempted by Satan;
He was with the wild beasts;
and the angels waited on Him. (Mk 1:12-13)
But if it is by the Spirit of God that I cast out demons,
then the kingdom of God has come to you. (Mt 12:28)

"As My beloved followers, you should know this:
I, when I am lifted up from the earth,
will draw all people to Myself."
"Won't You, then, Rabbuni, sustain us today
in our desire and endeavour to do You proud by our loyalty?
It'll be an enthusing assurance for me and others
that You will do all You long for us in Your faithfulness
for the simple reason that You delight in our faithfulness
and want our faithfulness to be more than a shadow of Yours!"

At dawn

Lord, as I accompany Your exercitants the time has come for me
to urge upon them the necessity of the choice they have to make
in response to whatever choice You've made for them. In my own
experience I know I've struggled hard to make my life choices.
Looking back I wonder if I had had enough freedom to make any
worthy choice. I'm afraid I am not very exceptional in this matter,
going by the desertions in priesthood and religious life in the wake
of Vatican II and also by the devious life of those who have not
quitted. If, with such a past behind me, I am in need of redemption
how am to help others who may be or could be as much trapped

131

as I, even if not more trapped? Of course, I've known, too, the marvels of freedom and choice of more people than I had believed. As I rejoice over their good fortune, Lord, how shall I accompany the less fortunate ones in their struggle to be true to themselves and to You?...

Lord, were Your first disciples more free than I or those I have to deal with, Lord? And whatever choice did they make individually with regard to their life? What remained of their choice at the end? This sudden flash of questioning rising within me gives me a respite from the rash of possible despondency! But, what is more, You don't leave us to our own weak, frail and immature choice. You refine, rather, our steps to our freedom and enable us to live in a way that reflects Your love and power.

Lord of our free destiny, I realize that the Exercises do not stop at being devotional; they pass on and press on to combat ... in the spirit of what You Yourself said: "Do not think that I have come to bring peace to the earth; I have not come to bring peace, but a sword" (Mt 10:34). The sword of division ... sword of decision! Can our weak hands wield such a sword ... especially turned to ourselves, with fears hard to face and habits hard to break? Can our timid hearts survive their struggle and reach a decision against our peer patterns of thinking—clearly wrong, and woeful and worldly wise? Not unless You have been laying the foundation for the kind of maturity that is required for all this. With confidence and courage that come from You alone, we want to take one step at a time in this decision process ... whether it is the first or umpteenth time in our life. At the end, Lord, *"pone me iuxta Te;* give me a place beside You,"[240] as Ignatius prayed. Otherwise I'm afraid I'll willy-nilly end up shamefully sheltering from the light, if not extinguishing the light, that dispels the darkness of sin and death!

During the day

Lord Christ, what history of mystery—a mystery of the real—do You reveal here? The background of the mystery goes back to human origin and the foreground brings near human redemption. As You called forth every human person to exist in Your creative providence, You want everyone to be active under Your standard in Your redemptive ambience; and accordingly You call everyone to carry Your banner. Everyone like me and so me too. This double mystery is clear enough as a thought, but hardly grasped. Whoever grasped it could not only say, "What is a human that you give a thought to the small creature?" but also serve Your glory in the work of Your redemption. Oh, that Your will be done on earth—in me and mine—as in heaven, visible and invisible! You know if this wish arises from a heart that desires to act in response to Your call as Saviour despite my conduct till now.

In opposition, Lucifer issues his own calls—that pathetic, deceptive carrier of light that does not even glimmer, let alone lighten. This negative intrusion too is clear enough; but despite its dark performance, is often enough inviting, insidiously inviting, if I go by the general run of humanity, sadly enough including me—You alone being the sole exception, and after You Mary our Mother.

All of human living, whether individually or collectively, in the past or present or future appears to be a dramatic struggle between good and evil, between light and darkness.[241] We are used to speaking of Two Standards, Christ's and Satan's. But it is odd when we come to think of it; it strikes me as enormously wrong to use the same word in relation to You and, let me say in another breath, also Satan. Such usage bespeaks a certain alliance of ours in the past with its hangover. We have lived believing Satan is sugary and pleasing enough and indeed more pleasing than not; and no wonder You've found us not easy to please. That is how matters stood for us in actual life. Or, at least, that is how we have continued our important matters and affairs of life.

But now I shudder to realize the kind of terminology we've been using unthinkingly. And so now to think of You or refer to You in a terminology that grasps Satan too or vice versa I shun! Can light and darkness be grasped by one and the same terminology? Does not the first negate the second?... Though not vice versa ... and this is important. Because the second doesn't exist in the same way; ontologically evil has no existence of its own, no reality, no reality in its own right!

In this light, surely, the opposition staged and waged by Satan in our world history does not evoke or bear any intrinsic comparison ... with the unique drama of Your life, at once intimate and universal, in which You offer to programme us as Your disciples.[242]

If he opposes any at all it is us humans! Humans carrying out our part—the saving part—of the divine 'curse': "I will put enmity between you and the woman, and between your offspring and hers" (Gen 3:15).

And how divinely 'lucky' we are to find a way to arrest the advance of the camp of Satan and even beat it back and vanquish it! A way that You teach, the way that You Yourself are in very life, at once convincing and compelling, though also conflicting with our inclinations. "The genuine life" (# 139.2)! Would that we were received into this life (# 147.1-3) ... and became part of this life, the only life worth its name with all that it unfolds! Whatever life we had ... or thought we had ... in our ontological and spiritual poverty of dependence and degradation[243] clinging to any creature comfort or tangible good and tempting honour ... we now want to lose and let go in You. So we would ally with You ... and align with Your direction ... and live with You!

But what of our bruised and bloodied life in Eve and Adam who thought they followed their bliss?

You made Paul understand it ... and led him to explain it. "Adam prefigured the One to come," he found himself saying; "but the gift itself considerably outweighed the fall. If it is certain that through one man's fall so many died, it is even more certain that divine grace, coming through the one man, Jesus Christ, came to so many as an abundant free gift. The results of the gift also outweigh the results of one man's sin.... If it is certain that death reigned over everyone as the consequence of one man's fall, it is even more certain that one man, Jesus Christ will cause everyone to reign in life who receives the free gift that he does not deserve, of being made righteous.... When law came it was to multiply the opportunities of falling, but however great the number of sins committed, grace was even greater" (Rom 5:15-20, JB). Lord, what is this more, the *magis* of Your doing ... that Paul speaks so convincingly of, just as You gave him to understand and utter?

Lord, we are used to speaking of the fallen world, and also of the redemption of the fallen world, but not so much of the redeemed world. Are You providing us another perspective? Or aren't You? To conceive the world of our experience as redeemed ... rather than as fallen ... whatever may be the apparent, glaring picture of our ordinary human imagination or limitation?

Lord, it is perhaps part of the deceit and subtlety of Satan to take us in with an untrue picture of the world as if it were without a Saviour. The truth is that, once redeemed, the world remains redeemed by You and so is necessarily always being redeemed not only in us but also through us. And so even if I had to "speak of Satan and the spiritual warfare that permeates my life and, indeed, all sectors of society where loyalty to God is a serious concern",[244] I would all the more attend to and rejoice in Your Spirit that renews our universe. I believe, therefore, that when Your Holy Spirit convicts me enough of my sad story of pride in riches and desire of the eyes or the flesh (1 Jn 2:16) the same Spirit converts me so that I may help in the conversion of others like me. Also as She convicts the world of antichrist (1 Jn 4:3) with its roots of pride, prejudice, hatred, violence, wanton destruction, etc., may I be rid of all its baneful influence and enter Your redemptive sphere not only to enjoy it but lead others to it.

Lord Spirit, may I dwell within Your aura; then I'll be safe from the danger of being drawn into the vortex of the world of self and sin and Satan. Blowing as You will carry me and land me with Jesus to be of help to Him as a redeemed person to testify to the truth of redemption, and walk the way of redemption. Here is the centre of redeeming life: here is where I seek myself to be received, here is where I would find myself placed, here is where I stand ... whatever I do. I beg You, Father, through Mary and Jesus, that I may be placed with Christ and be given a place in Him. Shall I then hope You would thus reveal Your Beloved Son in me and introduce me to all the dimensions of His quiet word to me and transforming deed in me? Then I will have a reason in the region of my heart, urging me to the tasks of Abba's reign on earth doing God's will in the way of Jesus and in union with Jesus.

At night

To yield myself, Abba God, to Your working in me and to prove to myself, Abba Father, that I understand what I've been praying for and also that I'm seriously interested in praying so, I'd like to prattle my intended leanings, that You taught Your favoured souls. I hope my prattle will become a prayer!

"As you wish, My daring one, I will put in your lips the same words that I placed in those of John of the Cross!"

Let me then dare pray his "crazy" prayer, sharing and echoing the same sentiments You granted Ignatius.

> I'd always seek for preference ...
> not the easiest but the hardest ...
> not the most charming but the most boring ...
> not what pleases but what repels ...
> not what consoles but rather what afflicts ...

not what saves us trouble but what gives us trouble ...
not the most but the least ...
not the highest and most precious but the lowest and most despised ...
not the desire of something but the non-desire ...
in fine, not what is better in things but the worse ...
thus putting myself in denudation, emptiness and renunciation of all
that exists in the world...
for the sake of Jesus Christ.

Having found this prayer surprisingly in the Sunday Magazine of
The Hindu, I don't want to be wanting in sensing its worth! I cannot
deny this to be part of the discipline of discipleship. So I have faith
You'll bring it all to pass leading me to a certain maturity ... and
ensuring my place by the side of Your Son, Jesus the Christ.

For I know You have done such works of grace not only in
obviously saintly souls but also in unsuspected souls ... like the
famous, but anonymous, confederate soldier who acknowledged
Your work in him and is known by his famous confession ... or
like the nobodies of the convent world. Are they not all interceding
for me? So I wait for Your great, gracious consolation sweetly
dispensed to me by Your intercessors.

I specially rely on the intercession of Mary, who found herself
placed by the side of Christ in His humble origin and His humbler
ending—that is, under what would later become the standard of
the Cross. Mary, my Mother, you come across to me as the shining
embodiment of the victory over Satan and the world. And you
know, as none of us does, how the devil or Satan, the seducer of
the whole world, wages war on your children, on those who keep
God's commandments and give witness to Jesus (Rev 12:17). And
so, who can intercede for me better than you that I may be an
intimate, not marginal, companion of your Son, Jesus, a genuine
imitator of His, yes, an inner disciple of His?

Abba Father, even in the understanding of the Two Standards the
devil, "the noiseless file"[245] can be at work and make us

misconstrue. I was shocked to find one such instance. It is not for me to construe coolly, as some seem to do, that not all the forces that work against God's action in us draw us to evil. But the truth is that the enemy of good is not evil but the less good! And so let me be vigilant to detect the hidden agenda of the evil one. Save me from such sharp and clever deceits of Satan and guard me with the enlightenment of Your Son's ways. Enable me to deal with them with the singleness of purpose as Your Son, Jesus, did when He was challenged only to be successful in His mission; let me succeed in His fashion. May I counter the desperate ventures of the evil one with the admirable adventures of Christ leading us and going ahead with Your programme. With Him we are sure to land the victory.

21. YOU ARE A CLASS APART!

Not everyone who says to Me, "Lord, Lord,"
will enter the kingdom of heaven,
but only one who does the will of My Father in heaven. (Mt 7:21)
Do not quench the Spirit. But test everything;
hold fast to what is good. (1 Th 5:19-21)

"My beloved, you do not belong to the world,
but I have chosen you out of the world."
"And so, won't You, Rabbuni, sustain us these days
in being proud of our new discipleship—nicely new?
It'll be a warm, effective assurance for us
that You will do all You want for us as disciples
for the simple reason
that You're more proud of us than we of You!

At dawn

"My beloved, I want our relationship to be wide, all embracing, leaving nothing out of the web, the warp and woof of your life!" Thank you for telling me Your wish, Jesus, in Your goodness. Steady me when pulled by vagrant wishes and anchor me in Your wishes for me. Good Lord, I wish that You save me from being goody-goody. Free me from seeming goodness, wordy goodness, simulating goodness, deceptive goodness, repelling goodness, judgmental goodness, unfocussed and therefore erring goodness! Can't there be an unambiguous goodness of pure Yes to You with no taint whatever of No to You?

Lord, in You everything was an *Āmā*,[246] a Yes to Abba Yahweh. Your name itself—perhaps the last of Your names—is rightly

139

Amen, Yes (Rev 3:14). May I, Lord, have the courage of conviction to profess and practice the *mantra* of Yes, after You, in Your manner? Is there any other way of being true even to myself, Lord? Let alone to You. That I may truly mature in the Spirit, it strikes me, even as You bless me You won't pamper me in my wishful thinking or half-hearted endeavour or even much labour without love at labour! And so I must stand by You wholeheartedly and be steadfast in the pursuit of You, who have already found me, believing in me more than I do myself!

During the day

"My weight is my love. Wherever I am carried, my love is carrying me."[247] Am I, Lord, as the saint, the converted sinner, felt he was? My livery too is my love; and so nothing even minimally can diminish the likeness of mine to my love! May this prayer of mine be true enough to prove my credentials as a disciple with an intense burning desire (*abhipsa*) for the incomparable You, surrendering all to You so that I may find in myself a new vibrant being.

Lord, I wonder if You were ever confronted with what the three classes of people have to deal with.

The three classes are simply all of the good people ... the mass of respectable people ... depending on the kind of intelligent, if emotional, choice they make and continue to make ... regarding what we find ourselves possessing rightly or, worse still, what we find one day surprisingly possessing us.

Who can claim to be in such a good club? Or, how many of us? ... Even now ... in the course of the Exercises now? Or, even after doing the Exercises many times, year after year?

We have all something or other which we have succeeded in acquiring ... or managed to acquire ... or, of course, keep aiming and striving to acquire for ourselves. What we thus acquire we claim as our own. Whatever we have acquired—be it money or degree or position or achievement or excellence or even a person (though a person as such can't be acquired and so making it at least in this case intrinsically wrong)—we attach to ourselves ... instead of letting it be turned and oriented to You, while enjoying it and at the same time remaining ourselves attached to You. Our acquirement does not remain merely acquirement subject to us but subjects us ... encroaching into our very selves ... destroying the freedom of ourselves ... and so making it impossible for us to be our real selves and real persons—namely, the Father's generative acquirement and the Redeemer's redemptive acquirement and the Sanctifier's cherished, treasured acquirement.

In this, Lord Jesus, You are different, in fact the very opposite of us. You are indeed the embodiment of dispossession of everything that we allow to possess us. You are the incarnation of every despoliation that despoils us of our worth and existence, of our freedom and happiness.

But Lord, with regard to Your human life You did experience a desire to cling to life, something that is an existential inevitability at the time of danger to life. In this existential anguish of Your human self, or in spite of it, You seek to will and not will only as Your Father is inclined. With You can I say: "Not my will, but Thine be done"? When I hesitate to say, would You not say it in me, for me?

So in the face of life and death, of how it is to be and how long, etc., You are a class apart and You would want to number us with You in the third class, the class of the few, the class of the mature and strong. Would we not follow suit? How You strive to conduct Yourself as if existential attachment is broken ... is sundered ... because You are first and foremost surrendered to Your Abba. The truth of Your living is in Abba, Your attachment to Abba.

Lord, grant me the grace that I may desire ... know ... and so choose what is more pleasing to Your Divine Goodness. Your Divine

Goodness cannot intend or will what is bad for me. With regard to my attachments I need not even assume that the giving up of something that I like is necessarily Your will. Also, I need not, indeed ought not, to presume that what is more painful is all the more indicative of Your holy will! I sense Your inspiration in what someone has said so rightly: "You need not discard your possessions; it is enough to throw away your possessiveness."[248] So in this spirit of dispossessing my possessiveness I ask You to make me feel Your will and good pleasure ... to make me desire it ... and so to make me choose it ... so that Your wish and will become my own.

The world must be brought to know that I too, like You, Jesus, love the Father and that I too do exactly what is pleasing to the Father (Jn 14:31), indeed whatever is more pleasing to the Father.

So, dear Lord, I'm not simply interested in some salvation psychological or otherwise but radical salvation; so I ask myself, "Shall I be among the group of those content with velleities, the half-willed persons who play with compromise, or shall I be among those decisive persons who accept the challenge?"[249] To ask so is no more than a sensible grace, but no small grace and indeed no cheap grace.

What I want however is a big grace, and necessarily also a costly one too! The indifference par excellence! Á la Saint Ignace! Not merely a strong natural will power that is conspicuously absent in the general run of the first two classes. But beyond it, the power of the will collaborating and cooperating with Your grace. And so I look for and long for the singular grace that accomplishes Your work, the supernatural work in us.[250] Lord, is it not You after all who, for Your own loving purposes, put both the will and action into us (Ph 2:13)? So may it please You to bestow on me the grace that works, the grace of the third class: namely, the desire to be able to serve You better ... the desire that will enable me to overcome the affections in the sensitive part of my nature for any doll or idol of any created good ... the desire to throw away my possessiveness.

I'm really surprised to think that the affection for the created good need not be and indeed is not less strong in the third class than in the first two classes. I'm more surprised that a superior spiritual affection, the fruit of grace, comes in—oh! how I wish it rushes in—to establish an equilibrium between my desire for Your will and my desire for a creature gift which I don't wish to part with. What a gratuitous grace it is! A grace that adds a new weight to the inclination of my will itself! "My weight is my love; by it I am carried wherever I am carried." And surely You, my God, weigh more than all the world put together,[251] in particular the world of fame and success!

At night

St Ignatius, I pray for the elusive grace of being and doing what I know. In the novitiate Father Master John assured me of the grace I enjoyed of being trained from my teenage in the Society. I am sorry that if I've learnt much I haven't done much! So I'd like to learn again to pray with you:

> Teach us, good Lord, to serve You as You deserve; to give and not to count the cost; to fight and not to heed the wounds; to toil and not to seek for rest; to labour and to ask for no reward, save that of knowing that we do Your will.

22. WHEN HUMBLED

God did not give us a spirit of cowardice,
but rather a spirit of power
and of love and of self-discipline. (2 Tim 1:7)
All of us, with unveiled faces,
seeing the glory of the Lord as though reflected in a mirror,
are being transformed into the same image
from one degree of glory to another;
for this comes from the Lord, the Spirit. (2 Cor 3:18)

"You should know, as My dearly beloved,
you are not greater than Your Master:
If they persecuted Me, they will persecute you."
"When humbled won't You, Rabbuni, remind me
of being in good company, Your company,
Your privileged company?
It'll be a comforting assurance for me
that I won't be stranded or side-lined or sunk or suppressed.
Rather You'll do what You desire in Your glory
enabling even shaky me to stand by You,
stand empowered in Your aura!"

At dawn

Do "we owe subjection and humility to every creature for the love
of our Lord"? Blessed Peter Faber said yes as You had taught him
surely after Ignatius, as also Benedict and Bernard before him.[252]
After all, that is how You conducted Yourself, Lord, from the very
beginning of the Passion right through to its end. Your kind of
humility, then, signifies more than resignation; it means

144

submission, a submission to reality, the reality of God that includes all so-called reality even of inhumanity. Such submission is expressed in properly ordered love (*ordo amoris*) with a sure orientation to goodness as it looks finally to God who is good, yes who alone is good. Humility is therefore an experience of loving God first above all other beings; such humble love leads to the love of every earthly reality whether of oneself or other humans or other things in that order, far from natural but properly supernatural. If humility is such an attractive thing attaining it may not be so; it may involve hard lessons. Learning from You St Bernard could say: "As patience leads to peace, and study to science, so are humiliations the path that leads to humility."

Not a common ambition, but a magnanimous choice among Your lovers who would grow in resemblance of You little by little, never seeking glory or vainglory nor nursing bitterness about harm done. Did women saints excel in this respect more than men saints? St Gemma Galgani would ask Jesus not to let her do things that are above her; St Germaine Cousin, despite all ill-treatment by her stepmother, asked God for grace to love her and please her. As You taught them in their typical ways I want to learn what You would teach me in this regard.

Is there any relation between humility and freedom? I discovered St Julia in this context. Though of noble birth she was enslaved by her captors only to recognise her noble character. When a prospective buyer offered her freedom if she would deny Christ she refused his freedom, claiming she was as free as long as she could serve Jesus. For all the fascination of the thought of freedom its reality is not a little frightening. It conjures up a state of mind in which one finds oneself having nothing to lose; in which one indeed has nothing to lose. It is simply the indifference (of the Principle and Foundation), the indifference with a difference. At this stage of the retreat, dear Jesus, it demands a sort of nakedness to follow You who were stripped naked.

"My beloved, I know you've gone through no small struggle. Still I'm happy you yourself have come to such a realization of this."

If only, Jesus, we could hear You whisper so in our silences and silent struggles we would be well stretched towards You. Anyway, for much of our life we go on avoiding this clear, unimpeachable path of life. At a certain point, however, as at this juncture of the Exercises we can no longer ignore it but confront its exigency. Victimized we have lost not a little; and yet here am I now drawn to You and enabled to give up the little that remains.[253]

"That is the way, My beloved, to launch into the deep, the deep relationship of love! What depth of love can you enjoy unless you dive deep, leaving ashore all fear?" So true, Lord. I wish I could say, like St Gemma Galgani, for example, who could say to You simply: "I look only for You; I want only You; do not doubt that your Gemma will follow You to Calvary."

"Dom, as a help to activate your wish, I give you this personal antidote: 'The insults of those who insult you have fallen on Me' (Ps 69:9; Rom 15:3)."

During the day

Lord Jesus, I begin this prayer with a great consciousness that there is a great chasm. I feel I am far away from You, if certainly not You from me. This feeling makes me feel everything futile; it is an oppressive, crushing experience. If You let me remain so maintaining Your silence of no response I am doomed and no one will do or can do anything. So I am afraid, Lord, afraid of You, of Your punishing me, of Your apparent scheming harm.

Lord, I feel so humbled, so much brought low, so very helpless, so very lifeless ... I wonder how I can pray in such a situation.

In this situation when I feel I have been hounded out and exposed, what do the three degrees of humility mean?

Whatever variety of humility Ignatius has proposed from his experience—that was something granted him by You, the beneficent Lord. He learnt from You the basic meaning of humility. His vision of humility was no small enlightenment of his mind and heart from You, the Father of lights. Thanks to Your illumination, humility appeared to him no abstract virtue. It appealed to him as a personal relationship between a human person and the divine person of majesty, as each one is. Yes, a relationship bridging positive infinity between Creator and creature. Lord, You don't allow the work of Your hands to negate itself by virtue of humility. Rather, You enable it to be what it started to be from Your breathing life into it.

Whatever may attract or influence me or impinge on me, may I not destroy Your creative relationship with me in any serious matter or situation. May I not be the one without God, without my God, without the God of my life. May I not become Godless, devoid of life and meaning and reason for existence.

Even in small matters may I not countenance any decrease in Your sphere of influence. May I not be related to any existence more than to Existence itself, that is, to Your Existence, that is, to You. May I know nothing else more pleasing or pleasurable, more satisfying or satisfactory, more engrossing or enthralling, than You. May I be so humble that I preserve the pure tie between You and me and keep myself free from the knotted ties that can keep me bound and fettered away from You.

Lord, in so maintaining my original relationship with the Origin that is You, can I preserve Your likeness in me better than in imitating Your own beloved Son Jesus – the Link of all relation with You? And he was ill-treated, humiliated and made to undergo all evil. Likeness to Abba God and His Son, if it means anything, it means only one thing—the third degree of relationship with Jesus, a relationship that looks to similarity, even identity, and in the process dares risk everything like Him and gambles on His

Abba! Humiliation can then sound the measure of our greatness; though usually it parades human pettiness or meanness it can become a revelation of our new features, divine features of Christ.[254]

But, Lord, what does all this mean for one who feels he is all cut off from You? Well, let me rest in myself in simple, helpless humility; and what is more, thanks to lofty humility—Your lofty humility—let me rest in You hoping in what You alone can do in us who have to learn humility with every humbling experience.

For I believe humility is Your spiritual doctrine "which is spiritually received in the closet of the soul (only) by those who are counted worthy of it".[255]

At night

Saint Augustine once wrote "Only through the degrees of humility can one reach heaven. God is infinitely perfect, and pride keeps us far from Him, but through humility we are able to approach Him."

And so St Francis De Sales could counsel and encourage: "The highest point of humility consists in not merely acknowledging one's abjection, but in taking pleasure therein, not from any want of breadth or courage, but to give the more glory to God's Divine Majesty, and to esteem one's neighbour more highly than one's self."

When humbled, where is Your will, Abba? What is Your will for me? Of course, there is the question: what is Your will for the offending person? But for the moment I'm peaceful to consider Your will for me when offence is done by the offender.

I can accept Your will as a negative norm, telling us not to do something bad even when treated badly and, more generally, to remain within certain bounds, as most of the Ten Commandments bid us. Abba God, I can take Your will as a positive norm, inspiring and inclining us to Your kind of choices and so proving and confirming our conversion from addiction to money or fame or pride ending in sin. I can recognize Your will as more than a norm and embrace it as embodied in *a life*, in someone living fully, the person after Your heart—in Your Son Jesus Himself who is Your will for us. Can this will in flesh and blood sway us, Abba, and swoop us away and sweep us into Your bosom, humbled and at the same time exalted, establishing a harmony in my soul, humble and confident? Then I'll bear His visage and image! With its aroma of dignity, grace and nobility—the aroma whose fragrance is however only savoured in poverty, suffering, humiliation and even death. "I should hope to be so poor, to suffer so much, and to be consumed by the sanctity of the Christ that in the end I would not even flinch at the assault of death's blow to my body."[256]

23. A METHOD IN MADNESS

The wind blows where it chooses, and you hear the sound of it,
but you do not know where it comes from or where it goes.
So it is with everyone who is born of the Spirit. (Jn 3:8)
If you are reviled for the name of Christ, you are blessed,
because the spirit of glory, which is the Spirit of God,
is resting on you. (1 Pet 4:14)

"I am at once Master and Servant."
"Won't You, our sole Master, help me this day
in our burgeoning, if as yet hesitant desire
for close discipleship in Your servanthood?
It'll be a tremendous boost for me
that You will bring to fruition Your will for us
for the simple reason there is no way otherwise!"

At dawn

Lord Jesus, only You can be humble because You alone are in point
of fact that great, overwhelmingly great, so great especially in love!
If so, the degrees of humility are really degrees of greatness! I pray
reasoning so, not to excuse myself for not being humble ... or for
being humble in a peculiar sort of way! You know, Jesus, I feel
like saying I'm humble in myself, but not in relation to or the
presence of the proud! That is being selectively humble! Anyhow,
wanting to be truly humble in myself like You, I still wonder if I
can ever be humble like You. For, I have heard it said: "Don't try
to be humble; you are not that great!"[257] It would seem only the
great can be humble; there is much wisdom in the saying: "The
greater you are, the more you must humble yourself" (Sir 3:18).
You had Your own dignity; and, relating to us, You lowered Yourself

150

to our level; You let go Your dignity. That is what seems to us but to You, I wonder, if it was undignified. There is then dignified humility, is there not, my Lord? The humility of God-Man is humbling and yet uplifting because of Your very holiness ... Your very dignity! Can this be, Lord, or indeed can't this be, "the true distinction—to have no distinction at all"[258] among ourselves but be like You, humble, without the visibility of Your dignity, and so serving and so even disposing of Your life as a slave.

If I am not great enough to be humble, I want to be like You in Your humbled state because otherwise I would only be ashamed of myself. Of course, I wish I could say I'd share something of Your humiliation because I loved You. If I loyally love You and do not only think I love You there is only one way of proving it for myself, if not You. The proof of the pudding is in the eating. The proof of my love is in my being with You, sharing with You, imitating You and becoming like You! In particular like You in Your suffering and affront, thus becoming vulnerable and so letting pain flow into our lives and not being cool enough to be skilled in avoiding it or even undergoing it stoically. Won't You make this the law of my life inspired by my love, my grace of love, courageous, if foolish, love of You?[259] In Your footsteps I want to march to the beat of a different drummer, the unusual kind of drummer.

During the day

Lord, thinking of the first degree of humility, I recall Your encounter in the desert. You had to face the devil's seduction of self-aggrandizing authority over all creation as it showed You all the worldly kingdoms in their glitter and haunting splendour. But You brushed aside the temptation all at once and dismissed the tempter unceremoniously without entertaining any thought about it or even entering into any deliberation. You so subjected and humbled Yourself as to obey Abba God and Lord in all matters ...

151

in all contexts and contingencies ... even to the point of being tempted by the Adversary. Your principle was clear: "You must worship the Lord Your God and serve Him alone."

Lord Jesus, thinking of the second degree of humility, I recall Your social experience of living with opposite contingencies. Your mental attitude with regard to such opposites as wealth and poverty, honour and dishonour, longevity and brevity, was one of simple, noble freedom. You were at home with either alternative as occasion needed and demanded. You did not always disdain the former, nor did You always court the latter. Just as You had it in You to befriend the poor so You knew how to keep the company of the rich too if that was the contextual way of doing good, the greater good. So also in the matter of honour and dishonour. You sought no approval of anyone, even of the high and mighty. Also, You could take it in its stride any dishonour or brush it aside; this was no unusual experience for You. But You were not afraid of honour either: when situation warranted it, You could accept honour too without any sense of guilt or foul pride ... yes, when good and divine sense directed and dictated it! Yes, divine sense— that is it! You were really indifferent to the opposites not caring for either, except of course when one or the other was clearly indicated to be for the greater service and glory of Your Abba God.

Lord Jesus, thinking of the third degree of humility, I realize that it is simply defined by Your very identity ... imparted and imprinted by the Father. You are identified as a poor man (having no place of Your own at least at Your birth, or during Your public exposure, or at Your death) rather than a rich man. You are associated with the humbled and the rejected with the unusual reputation of being the friend of the hoi-polloi and, in particular, the regular sinners like the tax-collectors or prostitutes and sinners caught red-handed. You came to bear even the name of a glutton and drunkard ... rather than a title of the élite. You were numbered among the unwise and unesteemed; You were made a fool and paraded so.... In all this it would seem You did not choose, or did not have to choose, such a way of life. It would rather appear that Your Abba God of divine majesty Himself chose You for poverty rather than riches, for humiliation rather than honour, for rejection rather than esteem, etc. Is it that the Father himself is thus, unimaginably, humbly disposed because of his infinitely high majesty of divinity? When, then, Lord shall I be cloyed with desire for honours and be clothed with becoming beauty of choice humility?

Lord Jesus, would You please lift me up high ... or, better still, let me see how You hold me so high ... so that I may freely ... and truly lower myself and humble myself and subject myself to You and Your Father and Your Spirit in the very world of my daily, concrete experience of life ... with all its currents and cross-currents and undercurrents? If this were to be part of my normal self there would be nothing to make me left wanting and feeling so gloomy and terribly sad!

Am I going back to the threshold, the preparatory stage of the Exercises? Or, better still, have I not to go back time and time again to the earliest foundational exercise, my Lord? Anyway ... is there any other way to find meaningfulness in the face of sinfulness that is total meaninglessness?

At night

The three degrees of greatness are the three degrees of humility. Are they not, Lord, also the three degrees of love? After all, can love resist falling on its knees?[260] Indeed, does not love feel comfortable falling on its knees, sinking on its knees? In that case, Lord, can the first degree exist without the second and, for that matter, without embracing also the third? How often unthinkingly we exclude the possibility of living according to the third degree! We take for granted the third degree is exceptional, beyond the reach of common souls.

Equally wrongly we take for granted that common souls can attain at least the first degree. How foolishly do we assume that, as in other cases, here too a lower degree can exist without the higher! But is not the truth different, Lord ... far different? For the truth is far more challenging: "The first degree can only be fully realized when the time comes for it to be exercised if there has been constant progress towards the third degree"![261]

To that extent who loves You ... who can love You? Only a rare person with a heart that has reasons of its own that reason does not know? But You came for all persons, calling all of us, addressing each one of us with the same message of love in life. When one believes in Abba God can one live for anything else but for Him alone? When we see You loving us and Abba even if it costs Your life can we count the cost in order to preserve our life? When one comes to think of it, how true it is that either all the three degrees of love exist together or none does. Does love calculate? Or ever think of calculating? It has no half-measures! Either it has all or none!

But what is the range of love in the present stage of my retreat? You know it, Lord! And I keep trusting that the freedom and the joy of Your Kingdom will overtake us sooner or later so that I may soon enough succumb to the options and preferences of Your career.

And I hear You answer my prayer with Your refined encomium on your beloved ones like Mary Ward: "To love the poor, persever in the same, live, dy and rise with them was all the ayme of Mary Ward".[262] The day has come—hasn't it, Lord—for me to go beyond lip service to such an ideal of integration and join them in life service?[263]

154

24. THAT WE MAY TRULY MAKE THE EXERCISES

To you it has been given to know
the secrets of the kingdom of heaven;
blessed are your eyes, for they see,
and your ears, for they hear. (Mt 13:11, 16)
When the Helper comes, whom I will send to you from the Father,
the Spirit of truth who comes from the Father,
He will testify on My behalf.
You also are to testify
because you have been with Me
from the beginning. (Jn 15:26-27)

"Devout souls, 'Take courage; I have conquered the world!'"
"Your words, Rabbuni, come as a balm today
when, reduced to our naked spiritual reserves,
we feel we have failed to make the grade.
Your bold words, however, lift us after touching bottom
and despite appearances to the contrary
more than recompense our misery.
Your self-assured words bring us to delight in Your success in us
for the simple reason that, though elusive, it is so sure!"

At dawn

It looks strange for myself, let alone others, but not for You, that I should pray in this manner half way through the Spiritual Exercises. But, dear Lord, I tend to believe You have a hand in making me turn to this matter. You will help me to understand—won't You, Lord?—so that together with the exercitants, I may shed my ignorance or inadequacy or presumption, and learn the way to become enlightened. Enlightenment is, like all consolation (# 316), not of my making but Your grace and gift (# 322).

I came across a difficult idea, namely *representation* ... and, along with it, there was *the challenge of going beyond representation* ... and *so attaining enlightenment*. But one thing is clear: humility will serve here so sensibly, even as I continue to set my sight on Your heights. Thanks to my littleness I'll count on You alone for everything!... And in particular, for access to You in inaccessible heights where no one can ascend unless You lift us up.

I am amused to think this is not unlike my boyish attempt at writing my diary. I remember the first time I jotted down the four or five words in my proposed diary: "I'll be a good child!" Was it the first *review* of my little life put in black and white, expressing my desire to be pleasant and win over the favour of others, especially *Amma* (Mom) and *Appa* (Dad)? Anyway, next time I jotted down something in the diary it was the same sentence! Unfortunately I gave up writing the diary after not many more similar, yes repeated, jottings! I wonder if it is the parable of my whole life ... and even of all human life, in particular of Jesuit life-print— doing something, say doing the examen, repeatedly because of the Ignatian ideal only to give it up after a decade or so because it does not seem to lead us anywhere, let alone higher! If this were true—though I wish I were wrong—is it because we have never learnt the truth by doing rightly and properly? Or is it because we were never truly converted?

Save me, Lord, from such wastage of pearls ... at least for the sake of the exercitants! May each exercise we do during these days of Your favour turn out to be a pearl ... the result of Your grace at work in us in and through or perhaps despite the friction of our exertion! May we shrink from cheapening what is precious and dear!

"My Beloved, you should not be so depressed about what seems to you a continuous, futile pursuit producing no flash of spiritual fireworks. I assure you nothing has been a waste. You must trust that out of what seems to be a huge mess your Papa God 'weaves a magnificent tapestry' for you and My retreatants. His are the *magnalia* and not yours. So when you feel lost as now 'you don't need to have it all figured out'[264] all at once. What matters is just being with Me always. Continue believing what you know: Who is with you, reaching out to you in a hundred and one ways (# 320)."

This word of Yours is a command of consolation to me to proceed on the way ahead of me, preserving myself in patience and cherishing with hope Your favour to come. I'll ever bear in mind Your reassurance: "Do not say, after spending a long time at prayer, that nothing has been gained; for you have already gained something. And what higher good is there than to cling to the Lord and persevere in unceasing union with Him?"[265]

During the day

Lord, as creatures, as works of Your hand we are representations, beings who are not our own origin, beings who are manifestations, yes merely manifestations, of something else, namely the original source. But in You, Lord, we are more than mere representations; aren't we, Lord? In Your created nature You too are a representation ... but not like us made in the image of God. In Your human bearing You are the Image of the invisible God and Father; and so You are the Representation which is identically the Reality! And so, in You and through You we are what You are, not in the same way but in some way!

Our Christian existential vocation in You, Lord, is to go beyond the representation as disconnected from its source, the initial motion which made it be. How do we do so, Lord? How do we transcend the representation? Not certainly by arriving at some conceptual concoction or conviction of truth even of the absolute order. You never indulged in such terminology. Is it not rather by wax-like sensitivity towards You and thus uniting ourselves to You, the Image, by welcoming the Image to be in us what it is, namely the Image who is You Yourself, the Son of God, and hence who is Your own Truth, unlike us?

God forbid that we live and pray within representations alone, without being stripped of all images (Mt 6:6).[266] For I understand: "To live within representations is to perceive mental images, external things, the words of the Bible, the events of salvation history, but without attaining by way of those representations the meaning."[267] But it is the meaning which would lead me and everyone of the exercitants to live in conformity with Christ.

Lord, is it right that most of the Gospel characters, namely the crowds, stay at the level of representations? They are delighted with Your stories, but miss their aim and fail to grasp their meaning. That is why, Jesus, You said in Isaian style: "You will indeed listen, but never understand, and you will indeed look, but never perceive" (Mt 13:14).

They never pause and ask themselves where they are with regard to the kingdom of God. Surely to transcend the representation towards its meaning is to live on the level of such a question, an existential question, and to work accordingly and shape life.[268]

Lord, do we, the exercitants and I, do that? You'll help us beyond what we think we need! In particular, won't You help me to help them? Help them obviously transcending me and even bypassing me, if and when necessary, as You please. But by the end of the Exercises may I myself be helped, Lord! May I find myself more than helped, Jesus!

After coming across this philosophical idea or problem of representation, I feel very inadequate to be busy with the Exercises. Is it true that many exercitants do not get further than representations? With a great deal of good will and fidelity, it seems they fill their imagination with images, words, etc., and yet nothing or almost nothing happens. *I shudder to hear the paradox that those who remain within the representational framework will have made a very good retreat, but ineffectually.* For the conversion hoped for does not follow! Or seldom if ever!

> Where do I stand, Lord? And my beloved exercitants?
> I don't feel elevated; I feel far from uplifted!
> But I like to go back to something very typical of the Exercises.

We are not in control; neither I nor the exercitants. Where we are ... wherever we are ... however we are ... sure or unsure of ourselves, flying up in the sky or plunging down in the depths, there You are; and You deal with us directly (# 15:6). In Your accustomed ways You enter the soul, move it, draw it toward Yourself (# 330:1), grant it an abundance of sorrow, overflowing love and intensity of Your favours (# 320:3), bring its desires into order (# 16:5) and so communicate Yourself, even to the point of embracing us (# 15:4)—raising us thus beyond mere representations. Accordingly I beg You to be pleased to move our will and to put into our mind what we ought to do in the different matters of choice (# 180.1).

Apart from You, we are nothing especially spiritually and can do nothing. "To embrace this precious nothingness is to make (You) Jesus all in all."[269]

And I sense what You say to me: "Do not feel, after spending a long time at prayer, that nothing has been gained; for you have already gained something. What higher good is there than to cling to the Lord and persevere in unceasing union with Him?"[270]

Given this faith in Your action during the Exercises, our repeated contemplations should be blessed by You, so that we find ourselves being confirmed in You and conformed to You beyond mere representation! Yes, Lord, this is my secret jolly prayer I join to the angels' (like St Peter Faber) who are continually in the presence of Abba (Mt 18:10); in Your loving patience—or is it jolly patience?—bring us into Your intimacy and save us from our naïve ignorance, stupidity, sorry discovery of confusion and confounding sin of presumption. What is more, You believe more in us than we in ourselves! Let me therefore be and learn to be in vigilant prayer, expecting and trusting that You'll do what You intend to! For, given our nature, we'll much sooner tire of receiving Your gifts than You of giving them.[271]

If the day brought me a crisis during the retreat it has produced no setback but a new awareness of Your primary role. Crisis serves as a cause, as a speciality of those who belong to You and want to know as they are known by You. I take pride as it is our *specialité de la maison.*

At night

Lord, there is always the right time for us, is there not? The time chosen by You, the grace of the eleventh hour surprising our endeavour or the lack of it (Mt 20:1-15). When, with all my futile strength, I find myself at the end of my tether it is not all defeat or loss but surprise stumbling into Your boundless resources (2 Cor 12:9). It struck me today that just before dawn is the darkest time of night—and so too the time of enlightenment comes after the time of darkness and disorientation whatever the cause. For the propitious time You prepare us even in spite of whatever we may be. As You did when You let Your disciples know that life is knowing You and Your Abba, You now choose to disclose it to us (Lk 10:21-22; Jn 14:5-11).

After hearing all that from Yourself, in Your hour of trial they behaved only betraying their belief. That makes me terrified about my behaviour. In this very terror I remember Your favour to Moses. Your Abba had allowed Himself to be seen by Moses whom He had prepared for the experience and who was also thus fitted to be the vehicle of transmission of the same experience.[272] Letting go my performance let me hold on to Your performing grace, Lord. So I ask earnestly: "O gracious and holy Father, give us the wisdom to perceive You, intelligence to understand You, diligence to seek You, patience to wait for You, eyes to behold You, a heart to meditate upon You, and a life to proclaim You: through the power of the Spirit of Jesus Christ our Lord."[273]

Praying thus is almost being reborn again. In this spirit I wish I never cease to be born again and again.

25. THE ORIGINAL EUCHARIST

It is the spirit that gives life; the flesh is useless.
The words that I have spoken to you are spirit and life.
But among you there are some who do not believe. (Jn 6:63-64)
I beg you to lead a life worthy of the calling
to which you have been called
bearing with one another in love, making every effort
to maintain the unity of the Spirit in the bond of peace. (Eph 4:3)

"Who is greater, My dear ones:
the one who is at the table or the one who serves?
But I am among you as one who serves."
"Won't You, Rabbuni, undeceive us
of all our unwarranted complacency in our following You
even as we try by ourselves to be self-aware?"
"Won't you, My beloved, be assured
that My loving knowing of you will prove victorious
for the very reason that you sense it
indispensable, if inaccessible, to you?"

At dawn

My Soul, smudged and ravaged by despicable choices, let us speak
to Christ bruised, though, by His daring choices: "Soul of Christ,
sanctify us. Body of Christ, save us." These are passionate
aspirations ... of a holy sinner. I wouldn't dare utter them by myself,
being what I am. But only knowing about You, Guru, in Your
forgiving love at the Last Supper, though still far from knowing
You in what You have done for us, I learn to repeat the prayer of a
sinner who learns to rejoice again and again as Abba rejoices in
forgiving us time and again.

Blessed are the souls, Lord, from which arose these hallowed words so spontaneously ... and yet not without being taught by You, the interior Lord. So, in or in spite of the dullness and hardness of my heart, I pray: may I learn harder as You teach me the hard lessons of love, as You demonstrate the love of Your Heart at the Farewell Meal with its unsuspected glimmer of Your Passion, shrouded in obvious pain and mysterious meaning that was not so obvious!

Eating that Meal, now become a New Meal for all times, in which You give of Yourself today I must draw my life from You. "Blood of Christ, inebriate me!" I have said so often and equally often with little or no understanding!

"My beloved, you loved to say those words; that is enough understanding, to be sure! Now I want you to understand more. Can anyone say to you: 'I love you so much, and in my love I desire that you draw all your life from me just as you do from your food'?[274] I know in your love with your intimate ones—babies or baby-like beloved ones—you felt drawn to bite gently even as you playfully say, 'I would like to eat you up!'[275] But that species of love, even at your dizzying heights of longing, you can't ever fulfil. But I mean to fulfil all that longing in relation to Me. Not that you have felt any such desire to eat Me up. But what nobody can say to you I do! I do mean that I love you so much; and so I want you to live wholly by Me as from necessary food or drink! It is as if food or drink were a person offering itself to you for your living at the times of your hunger or thirst! I know—whether you know it or not—that your food, real food am I without whom you cannot really live! And so I give Myself to you as food and drink that you can eat and drink! I am the substance of eternal life; if you believe and know it you will also know and believe that I am the substance also of your life, earthly and human."

Lord, I believe not only that You have the words of eternal life but that You are life, my life, indeed the life of the world! Jesus, with

Your blood fill me, fill all my veins, fill all the fibres of my being;
then I'll be exhilarated.[276]

'Ardent disciple, I would remind you of a piece of revelation you
stumbled upon in Abba's dialogue with a good soul. My servants
"find their nourishment at the table of desire, and they are at once
both happy and sorrowful".[277] Just as it began for Me at the table
of the last supper and reached its climax on the upturned table of
the most holy cross.'

During the day

At the Last Supper with Your disciples You tell them, "Where I
am going, you cannot come" (Jn 13:33). You reiterate it to Peter
in particular when he questions You where You are going. So You
discounted the probability of anyone of Your disciples going with
You and following You in Your Passion ... though You had wanted
them as disciples and followers to be where You were.

What about us, saving Master? My belief is that You do expect us
to follow You in the Passion, having led us thus far! That is why
You give us daily the Supper that refreshes and arouses and deepens
love![278] The same supper that You gave to Your distraught disciples!
Having said so I sense a doubt creeping in me. You knew Your
first disciples, Lord ... did You not? You knew they would not, in
fact, follow You through the Passion. Is that what You meant when
You remarked they could not be with You in Your Passion? If so,
what about us, Master? What do You know about us standing at
the threshold of the Passion?

Lord, we can't be too sure of ourselves; if we were we would not
be any wiser than Peter. Yet knowing that You have led us far
enough to make the choice of our life at this period of our life we
believe, Master, You'll lead us far enough into the Passion too.

It is in this light, Jesus, that the Last Supper emerges in my
contemplation. For one thing, if the original Eucharist is placed

at the juncture of the Second and Third Week it is "as the objective reality reached by the subjective conversion effected through the Choice."[279] For it is in, and not apart from, the conversion of bread and wine into Your own body-and-blood person that every personal conversion of ours takes on its full significance.

The original eucharistic conversion, indicated by the sacred words "This is My body ... This is My blood", signifies first and foremost Your free Choice of making a gift of Yourself to all humanity (## 195-196). With my own personal choice, can I not say something similar in imitation of You? So, with Your help, I say after You: "This (choice) is my body (from now on, my self and my freedom have no other body than this choice) which is given up for You (making me come out of my narrow confines and leading me into the universal community, and so sacrificing myself)."[280]

Your words of self-consecration "This is My body ... This is My blood ..." signify also the passionate sacrifice, the sacrifice of Yourself to Your Father for our sake (# 197). In this way the Last Supper embodying Your choice becomes "the very principle of all the mysteries that follow."[281] Thus, declaring Your will to sacrifice Yourself at the Last Supper, You begin Your Passion and commit Yourself to Your Passion and surrender Yourself in Your Passion. And what is more, You make Your Passion "a sacred action, the progress of the victim to the final immolation,"[282] and so a sacrifice indeed. Thus Your Passion just proves concretely Your choice words, unfolds the meaning of Your words of choice, realizes indeed Your words of intended sacrifice....

Such will be therefore the character of our own choice; no, Lord? There can be no escaping *that*, once we have made our choice, our free choice, our choice of our own accord. No wonder, then, You conclude Your sacrificial words bidding us: "Do this in remembrance of Me" (Lk 22:19)! So You invite us to express and experience, after You, our own choice we have made and so proceed to live by our choice, being true to our choice, walking necessarily the paths of the Passion and so in the manner of You.

This is becoming a live *Pietà*, like Your mother, and, more than her, like You, the pitiful One, the faithful One, not so much therefore the Man of Sorrows but the Man actualizing the choice externally, who loved at the Last Supper and so believed and lived it to the utmost till the end, the bitter end. Your pity or love knew no deception! And so You kept Your faith ... even to the point of proving Your Abba Father true at the height of the Passion when You felt forsaken by Him pitilessly!

It is with this faith, hope and love, sweet Saviour Christ, that I long for the presence of Thy very blessed body at the altar, and duly thank Thee for Thy gracious invitation and visitation to us, and further remember and consider Thy most bitter passion mysteriously enacted in the high memorial with tender compassion. "Make us all, good Lord, virtually participant of that holy sacrament this day, and every day. Make us all lively members, sweet Saviour Christ, of Thy holy mystical body, Thy Catholic Church."[283]

At night

Dear Jesus, with the Last Supper there is a new dimension to Your mystery, as it turns out to be the Everlasting Supper. If each and every event of Your birth and growth and work surpasses the historical moment and reaches us here and now, the Last Supper introduces a new dimension and adds a nuance to that unique experience of now, yes the longer now, the enduring now of the past promising the future. It was at the Last Supper, unlike earlier, that Your human experience itself melts into that subtler awareness of Your abiding presence for all time and history, bringing together the prophecy of the past and the receding future in the mystery of the present.[284] To You belongs love and that in power (Ps 62:11-12) as evidenced in the lasting fruit of the Last Supper. Is it because You are divine or simply because You are so perfectly human with an incomparable capacity for self-giving, despite Your vulnerability owing to Your love ... so attuned to Abba God's love? Anyway, Lord, the daily sacrificial meal or paschal manna is the perfect hope I have of ever knowing You, loving You and following You and thus becoming what You've called me to be ... in communion with not only You but "the many".

A nagging question, Lord, as we end the first day of the Third Week of the Exercises. Have we, Lord, really walked with You and arrived at the stage where we can really be where You are? And so contemplate You in Your Passion ... Passion that is part of Your Life? Isn't it true that whatever comes forth as a demand in our life proves to be no more demanding than our inherent, if unsuspected, strength is equal to? With all those who knew You in commitment I feel like saying now: "Only one feat is possible – not to have run away".[285]

"My beloved, you must know I let My disciples run away if they wanted to do. But I wanted them to stay with Me and watch with Me, praying as I did. That is what I want from you too: to watch the unfolding of My Passion of old and be watchful with Me in the primordial and perennial paths of My Passion."

Courageous Lord, bolster my courage, please, should I be wanting in love or boldness when I hear Your words of love even today: "I am ready to give My life again for you."[286]

Lord, I feel encouraged enough to be thankful. And I wait for Your favour: forbid that I become a party to the pathetic play of Your disciples in spite of their earlier protestations of loyalty, but daring to accept Your death as a strange gift You make to us, so that in some sense it turns out to be my own experience too.

Isn't it precisely what I'm doing when I receive in Communion Your Body-and-Blood-Self, saying yes to Your death as the sanctioned path to salvation in resurrection? And let me do so in the same spirit as You did—loving to the end: carrying to the end the plan of God of love and so reaching the beneficiaries even if they should, knowingly or not, reject it! When will the time come for me to intuit or believe that unearned suffering is somehow redemptive?[287]

Meanwhile, let me be still and know You are God even now; it is then that I'll know the why of my suffering—the sure way of fellowship with You, the Redeemer. Like your martyrs of old and even of today—whether they knew Your name or stood for Your cause of justice and truth. With them I pray: "Good Lord, give me the grace, in all my fear and agony, to have recourse to that great fear and wonderful agony that Thou, my sweet Saviour, hadst at the Mount of Olivet before Thy most bitter passion, and in the meditation thereof to conceive ghostly comfort and consolation profitable for my soul."[288]

26. SEASONED BY SORROW

Keep awake and pray that you may not come into the time of trial;
the spirit indeed is willing, but the flesh is weak. (Mk 14:38)
If you are reviled for the name of Christ, you are blessed,
because the spirit of glory and of power,
which is the Spirit of God, is resting on you.
On their part He is blasphemed,
but on your part He is glorified. (1 Pet 4:14)

"Dear loved one, do you know Me
as One who prayed with loud cries and tears,
to the One who was able to save Me from death?"
"So I dare ask You, Lord, 'Won't You help me this day
to sanctify my passion and passions all by myself with tears?'
Your sure help, and nothing else, will be an assurance for me
that You will do all You want for me in Your goodness
by virtue of Your sacred Passion.
I can then open myself to the cosmic passion
just as You did Yourself."

At dawn

"Behold the Christ, who shed His heart's blood for the redemption
of the world, who suffered a sea of anguish for love of all. It is
He, the master Yogi, who is in eternal union with Abba God. It is
Me and none other; it is Me, the Love incarnate."[289]

Good Lord, may we receive Your grace not to read or hear the
gospel of Your bitter Passion with our eyes and ears in the manner
of a pastime (as Thomas More so wonderfully prayed), even if it
be a pastime of prayer, but that it may become so present to us as

169

to draw our attention, the contemplative attention, "the loving attention that sees further than its eyes."[290] In this way, Lord and Servant of the Passion, we hope to draw close to the Reality, or better still to be drawn (as You draw us) close to the Reality of Your Passion as it appears in its contingency of human events and as it is in its mystery of the divine, of You, of Your Spirit and of Your Abba Father. So may we believe the Passion, and so may we live the Passion as You did, and become open to "a nobler life, where I may find the agonies, the strife of human hearts"[291] traced by You Yourself, Jesus, knowing fear, glorious fear, unlike soldiers unafraid of death! Yes, it can't but be that, as You focused Your anguish on ours, we need to reciprocate; and then it is that, in and through the very compassion of ours, Your redemptive power is released even in ourselves, and that not only for ourselves but the world. A "consummation of authentic compassion.... to be attentive only to others and to look on them as one would oneself.... to accept an active part in that drama which, since the Incarnation, is bringing humankind back to God."[292]

And so I would like to repeat what I sense Your *Imma* (Mom in Hebrew) is uttering in her agony with You: "I would rather / rather be here with You / than anywhere else / without You /... I would rather be mocked and ridiculed / with You / than be living comfortably / and well thought of / but without You /... I would rather / have You for my King, / crown of thorns and all, / than follow any other" (## 98, 157).[293]

Would that my heart felt what You'd gone through in Your Passion! "In the hour when You changed our fate, O Lord, You were quite alone. No one was with You; there was no comprehension and no love. Alone You carried our guilt before God's justice. But now You have taken us up in Your redemption, and I beseech You to grant that I know of You and be with You with my love."[294]

During the day

What is involved here in the contemplation of the Passion? The emotion of pity? Yes, no doubt about it; but not merely that. Beyond that and more than that here is "a faith that adores the God of majesty in the most divine of his works."[295] Because the various episodes of the Passion are all related not only to human wills but to the divine will! However much human figures dominate Your Passion—Judas with his betrayal, the Sanhedrin with its plotting, and the Romans with their playing safe in the political game—You in union with Abba and the Spirit are completely in charge of the whole unfolding of the Passion, suffering meanwhile the silence of Your Abba God to Your painful, tearful questioning and pleading.

Is that what Ignatius means by his mention of what You desire to suffer in addition to what You indeed suffer (# 195)? How truly You can speak of laying down Your life of Your own free will, will full of love! No one takes it from You. It is indeed the opening scene of the drama of the Passion as John, the favourite model disciple, saw and recognized it for himself (Jn 18:4-9). How well You had prepared for it! For all Your distress at the longed-for supper, You could breathe confidence and courage, knowing no one had power over You. And, at the same time, You could declare the truth of Passion: "I do as the Father has commanded Me, so that the world may know that I love the Father. Rise, let us be on our way" (Jn 14:31). So this singular love of Yours: that was the passion behind Your Passion! All humans have passion. Your passion was so different from our passions, holy or not so holy, let alone unholy. And so You could share a secret of Yours at one moment well before the Passion. "I have a baptism with which to be baptized, and what stress I am under until it is completed!" (Lk 12:50).

So can there be any compassion in Passion better than being one with You in Your passion for the Passion? Your raging passion for the fire to be lit on the cross (Lk 12:49)? Your urgent passion for that fire which alone can inflame human hearts? May my love so fill my being that it becomes an inner flame of love that spreads even outside singeing even my body as Your fire of love overflowed and singed Your body with wounds.

And so, Lord, during these days may the thought of Your Passion be my constant companion day or night and lead my heart to be attuned to Yours so that I'll be compassionate (Zech 12:10-11) ... as Your Abba.

At night

You hang crucified on the cross, Lord! Your crime is to have loved to the end! As You loved Your Abba to the end so did You love Your own to the end. If I were one of Your own I'd cry: *Amor meus crucifixus est*! My love is crucified! What is known to me of the old story of the Passion could dull the edge of the lasting mystery of the Passion. Save me, Lord, from so demeaning myself senselessly. Despite shameful temptation to lethargy now I want to be stirred enough to stay with You in self-forgetful love and self-awareness of my responsibility. "At this particular moment, my guilt appears so evident and conspicuous that it does not need to be brought to light; and on the other hand, in so far as it is mine it is insignificant, because only the burden it has placed on the Lamb of God is visible and of consequence."[296]

Now that You hang deformed on the cross, shall I not embrace You, Lord, in Your deformity? Or shall I be deformed, remain deformed, being ashamed of Your deformity? For Your deformity is no deformity but beauty, strange beauty, our beauty,[297] Lord, beauty of the union of Heaven and Earth, God and human, thought impossible by many.[298]

Here is the reason. Your divine Majesty stripped Yourself of all the grandeur of Your eternal glory in order to give us a share in it.

You took all our wretchedness upon Yourself in order to relieve us and free us from it. You desired to be sold in order to buy us back and so redeem us, to be abused in order to glorify us, to become poor in order to make us rich, to be led in pain and ignominy to Your death in order to bestow upon us a life of peace here and bliss hereafter.[299]

You had compassion for us first; and so we need to have it for You ... and equally for those who are in the same predicament and plight as You. So I can't avoid walking in solidarity with broken humanity ... broken in body, mind or spirit ... even should I lose a part or even the whole of my life! I was struck, though also put to shame about myself, hearing of a nurse who lived in such a spirit. At her funeral a Sikh reportedly said, "I've heard Christians say that Jesus died for our sins; I never understood it, though. But I know Stella died for our sins!"[300] This remark from a non-Christian reveals to me the depth of the familiar teaching on Your Passion by Your early and later followers. I am moved when I hear, for example, the encouragement of Francis de Sales: "Our Lord had not poured out His sweat and blood but that they should be mingled with ours, that these might win us the price of eternal salvation."[301]

Your Passion is the result and proof of Your Compassion to us, to me, indeed to all who have a mind and heart. Can our compassion be differently shown? If so, can our compassion stop short of real courage in the face of passion and suffering? To arm myself for my passion arm me with Your cross, as Miguel Pro experienced. Let me know this as my calling, as part of my calling as and when You choose me for it and make me aware of it.

27. THE HEART OF THE PASSION

Jesus bowed His head and gave up His spirit. (Jn 19:30)
One of the soldiers pierced His side with a spear,
and at once blood and water came out. (Jn 19:33-34)
I will pour out a spirit of compassion and supplication
so that, when they look on the one whom they have pierced,
they shall mourn for him, as one mourns for an only child,
and weep bitterly over him, as one weeps over a firstborn.
(Zech 12:10)

"You may say with Me, suffering soul,
'My God, my God, why have You forsaken me?
Why are You so far from helping me?
Where are You so far from the words of my groaning?'"
"Oh yes, Rabbuni Jesu, as I make Your prayer mine
help me to look also at the One Who was pierced for us.
It'll be an assurance for me
that Your wound will heal our wounds
for the simple reason that the scriptures affirm so!"

At dawn

As in everything about You, Lord of flesh and blood, Your cross is
the same as others'... and yet far different, by far different. It is
human and yet so holy, yes divine! If the death of Socrates carries
the marks of a sage, the death of Jesus with all its torment and ill-
treatment of remorseless executioners culminating in His forgiving
prayer is the death of a God.[302] Because You are the incarnate
Creator and Lord of all, Your cross stands in the very centre of the
history of salvation, and so of every human person's life-history,
and so, in particular, of our life, the exercitants' and mine.[303] And

174

thus is Your love revealed to us ... love that took our fate so much to heart that for our sake You Yourself incurred our fate![304] Let us, therefore, follow suit quickly, knowing that "whoever has suffered in the flesh has finished with sin" (1 Pet 4:1) like Christ—in His humiliation that is so much more than ours.

May this conviction, Lord, carry us through the contemplations of the successive mysteries of Your Passion, revealing in the process our own passion, right as well as wrong. And, so precious Lord, within our life that is so much of a paradox You'll draw us close to the paradox of Your Passion: all suffering passing under Abba's gaze before reaching Your soul.[305]

As I thus dwell on Your Passion in the background of my own, would You accept whatever pain of inward compassion arises from my depths as You grant me a newly awakening sense of shame for the sinfulness of myself first and then of others as well? Thus, Lord, I seek to be there where You worked out the salvation for all ... and for me ... and for everyone familiar with humbling state of living. Let me compose myself thus with the whole of my being, and connect myself to Your ever standing cross, using every little means ... even the composition of place itself as it is "intended to make each mystery of the Passion so immediately present that the exercitant feels that all this happened simply for him (or her) alone."[306]

During the day

Whatever You underwent in Your Passion, who could understand it all, Lord? Who can understand it at all? "They hated me without a cause" (Jn 15:25)! You said so, as You bared Your heart to Your disciples much perplexed by the events that overtook them as well as You. Words most human, giving utterance to the most human experience of God made flesh, exposing the vulnerability that is most like our own! Can You, Lord, be vulnerable? Even if God in flesh, should You be vulnerable like all flesh and go the way of all flesh? Yes, to be sure; and yet You were so notably and nobly different. Unlike us humans in our vulnerability, You in Yours absorbed the violence unleashed against You, and transformed it from within, and returned their hostility with gestures of caring, consoling, healing, forgiving, etc.[307]

Becoming flesh You embodied the glory of God for us! Abba God did make His divinity appear to us in You as His visible Image. Should He now hide His divinity in You? So we see You now dispossessed:

> without beauty, without majesty...
> no looks to attract our eyes;
> a thing despised and rejected by men,
> a man of sorrows and familiar with suffering,
> a man to make people screen their faces (Is 53:2-3).

God thus hid His divinity not only in You but also from You; or, so it seems to us! Why should He so hide His divinity—Your divinity—from You too? And You follow suit, leaving people to their own urges and devices of supposed choice that would not let You be You. With no holds barred they unleashed their rage on You, their blind fury against You, little suspecting You as the Lord of glory (1 Cor 2:8).

But we own You as Lord, missing though Your glory: the Lord of kenosis, of all loss, of nirvana, of becoming nothing.[308] You delivered Yourself to the powers that be with all power in Your very powerlessness just as they had planned to and, indeed would, take You as a brigand. Once in their hands You did not still hide Your divine relationship but chose to reveal Your true self in answer to their direct question about Your person, only to be condemned at once as a blasphemer. Is it not therefore they who hide Your divinity by their very rejection and ignorance? And sadly, how repeatedly it happens all through Your Passion as different characters encounter You. So do Judas and the whole crowd with him, including Malchus, in some slight form or other, experience

176

Your innocence and power, the human marks of divinity, only to ignore it or deny it in their own fashion. And how Pilate did so most! In spite of all that he sensed about You and Your innocence and perhaps something of Your heavenly origin, he came to the point of rejecting You, starting unwillingly, hesitantly and fearfully but finally ending it all desperately. In fact he sealed the rejection of You by all the others.

So the heart of the Passion is not so much that You hide Your divinity from the enemies but they hide it from themselves, from their experience, from their life, lest seeing it they should be forced to change their ways. They would rather go their ways, the way of rejection of Your divine way. There lies Your Passion.

In Your Passion You suffer rejection, not alone. Surely the Spirit of grace and truth too faces rejection (Mt 12:32; Heb 10:29). That is partly the meaning of Your sad words: "They hated me for no reason" (Jn 15:25). Further, in You and through You the Father too experiences rejection. If the prophet Samuel's rejection was the same as God's rejection (1 Sam 8:7), how much more so the rejection of You (Jn 10:34-39) must be that of Your Abba Father as well!

Such rejection of You, Jesus, sad and sorrowing, was not only once long ago, though You are no longer sad and sorrowing now. Unfortunately it continues today too ... because there are people who choose to reject You in their own fashion—and I am one of them, too, with all my shame hidden. So the situation that ensues from the act of rejection—whether by those of long ago or by those of the present—is one long uninterrupted Passion from the beginning till this moment. You are a God rejected then as well as now. That situation ... and not only the original historical act of rejection is the heart of Your Passion. How tragic that is, my lonely and so all the more lovely Lord of the Passion!

"We are made (thus in the Passion) to confront You, Jesus, in Your full humanity, and surely this does not diminish Your stature but rather enhances it. For this is a humanity that transcends any other that we know, a humanity so open towards the Father that, as we reflect on the events of the passion, we can believe with the early Christians that God was indeed at work here."[309] At work here as One who serves! Washing the feet of Your disciples at the Supper and yielding Yourself to be at the mercy of Your captors and surrendering Your life to those who demanded it!

Not only that; for, having been condemned as worse than Barabbas who was released, Your humanity descended far lower than ours in depravity and indignity. The worse was to come, as You cried out, "Eli, Eli, lama sabachthani." Like despairing souls, You seemed to be deprived of the mercy of God (Mk 15:31-32). Even though You continued to contemplate God even at Golgatha it was God lost to the sinners. You were so made into a sinner that You suffered the consequences of human sin that distance and separate sinners from God. As confirmed sinners end up by their choice to be without God, You could sense no comfort from God whom You contemplated facing only God's deafening silence. You could only be consumed by the opposition between all-holy God and all human sin that You chose to assume. Thus in Your Passion You descended the lowest depths of humanity—hell on earth—to be one with us and contemplate our situation and ransom us.

So we seek You there where You found humanity at its worst, and we want contemplate You in turn. And surprisingly enough, Yours is the divine majesty, become now for fallen humanity the veritable majesty of mercy and pardon ... so that the essence of fallen humans' service of the divine majesty is to be like You ... to be with You crucified![310]

As one who loved to the end You proved Yourself unique in Your love, not denouncing or demanding or distrusting, but humble and trusting and hoping. As a Lover whatever would You tell Your beloved? Would You ask them in their hearing, "Knowest thou yet what love meaneth?" Whatever would they answer? I heard one beloved murmur, "If I knew not the meaning of love, I should know the meaning of trial, sorrow and pain." Let me also belong to the circle of the Lover stretched on the cross to hear the voice of love and learn to make my personal response of love, as the conversation between the Lover and the Beloved continues to ring in my ears. "Knowest thou yet what love meaneth? If I knew not the meaning of love, I should know the meaning of trial, sorrow and pain."[311]

Your loud cry of surrender to Abba at the very end (Lk 23:46) rings out the message of Your prolonged pain and profound love. Are we not to see in this scene, like the good thief, Heaven opening— as earlier at Your baptism in the Jordan and at Your rising on the mountain?

At night

We have formally gone through the stages of purgation and illumination, Lord; and we have reached formally the Third Week of unitive life. Does this formal progress spell real progress, Lord? You alone can tell, Lord! We may only dare trust and hope!

In the third year of apostles' fellowship with You, they thought they were united with You but proved to be untrue to their own self-perception. I wonder if we are—or could be—different from them in this respect.

But, thanks to You, we can be different too. After all, there were some of Your beloved ones who stood with You and by You in Your Passion. If we were really in such a stage of union and love there would be no rules of discernment! No wonder, for the Third Week there are no such rules! Except love and the test of love. Love is discerning enough! Especially love purified and enlightened and illumined for two Weeks.[312]

Union with You in Your Passion is a rule simple enough to discern every interior motion or movement. The experience of such union is surprisingly, Lord, not so much suffering. You did not tell Your disciples at Gethsemane to suffer with You. You told them, rather, to stay awake and watch with You and pray beside You, like You, as long as You. May we not fail this test, Lord! Rather, may we prove ourselves disciples of mercy! Then You will make us witnesses of Your presence, like Dismas, the good thief, and Stephen, the proto-martyr.

Mother Mary to me: "Being a disciple of mercy is itself a vocation of all and so especially of disciples of Jesus. At the foot of the cross I did nothing but kept my heart open to my Son's suffering. Likewise be with those who suffer even if you can't remove their suffering; and then they'll discover, to their own relief, that being united with Jesus they can in their very suffering remain hopeful and even peaceful. Yes, that will happen if only you dare share their anguish in some measure and make your love visible and faith palpable."

And so, Mother Mary, let me learn to pray with you to your Son: "As You committed Your spirit to Abba God commit the disciples' spirits with Yours so that we'll all feel moved to follow You till the end with truth and loyalty." In this way and in no other, can we dissociate ourselves from all that depresses and drives us to despair, and so become free enough to commend our spirit to God!

28. ANY AND EVERY APPEARANCE OF THE RISEN ONE

Pray in the Spirit at all times. (Eph 6:18)
Without any doubt, the mystery of our religion is great:
He was revealed in flesh, vindicated by the Spirit
seen by angels, proclaimed among Gentiles,
believed in throughout the world, taken up in glory. (1 Tim 3:16)
If the Spirit of Him who raised Jesus dwells in you,
He who raised Christ from the dead
will give life to your mortal bodies also
through His Spirit that dwells in you. (Rom 8:11)

"Shalom, poor soul! I am Yehoshua Shalom.
Shalom rav (great peace)."
"Yehoshua Shalom, deal with me this day in my fragile faith
as with Your fair-weather, fearful disciples.
Only in that way and in no other
You can overwhelm me beyond what I do or not;
and You will do all You want for me in Your goodness
for the simple reason that You have faith in me!
And so may we receive a favourable hearing
when you move us to pray thus as fledglings in faith!"

At dawn

Mother of Jesus! Mother soaked in sorrow and wrapped in prayer, you knew to maintain your initial confidence till the end and so proved yourself a true partner of your Son (Heb 3:14). It was at the end you were to know undreamt-of befriending; it was at the depth of your sorrows that you were surprised by the unsuspected revelation.

181

No one knows the measure of your sorrow for your son, crucified and killed or what transpired in your sorrowing. However, your sorrow was human and we have an idea of it; it is not beyond our grasp. But no one can know what followed your sorrowful descent. You yourself could not have known of any ascent from depths of sorrow till you were surprised by your Son, Jesus. In your belief in God—for all your faith—you could see only darkly. No joyous mystery nor mystery of light could have prepared you for any glorious mystery. Much less your sorrowful mystery. But as in sorrow so in its sequence, there was a mystery, indeed a greater mystery, at once human and divine—so unsuspected, so unforeseen, so overwhelming, so unbelievable and yet so very real, indeed more than real. So, no wonder, Mother, "if we take the idea of a revelation of God in Christ seriously (as you did), then we must be willing (like you) to have our understanding of God corrected and even revolutionized by what we learn in Jesus Christ."[313] And this, in particular, in His Passion and Resurrection that reveal at once God's absolute judgment and redemption.

I've prayed to you, Mother Mary, for being placed with your Son, Jesus. If I were really placed with Him I would be found by your side too, in your personal loss because of His loss and in all that followed and overtook it. Looking at you I feel assured that we are not simply condemned to the sorrows of suffering nor the grief of the grave.

So I continue to pray to you, Mother, for being with your Son in an intimate way to the extent that He grants me as He granted you so uniquely: the grace of "a greater union with the crucified Lord in His risen life."[314] I want to know Him, Mother, and the power of His resurrection and the sharing of His sufferings by becoming like Him in His death (Ph 3:10).

Then I'll know to understand the past, free from pessimism and welcome the future with due optimism! Then I need not be anxiously struggling to forget the past, sad memories but remember their surprising, sudden forgetfulness thanks to the overwhelming memory of Jesus in His unimaginable joy.[315] Is there no way of abandoning myself to this joy?

Mary: "My son, there is: the way that I found myself walking, led by Jesus, always stunning! It was by way of an intimate apocalypse of grief turned to joy, fear to courage, terror to thrill, doubt to certainty, crushing love to ecstatic love. So why not try out yourself this exercise? Think a while, a long while as your love directs, on your Jesus, and see what happens for yourself, thanks to His love!"

Mother, from your own witness of love I desire and hope to see all shame removed, all losses restored and all sorrows ended. After all, the leaven of young adulthood of your 33-year old son was not lost but gave rise to a wonderful youthfulness of heart, fresher than Spring, with new, unsuspected resources, unwavering hope and overflowing joy.[316]

So I'll keep myself near Him, our Master. I'll keep waiting upon Him hopefully till one moment something stirs in me as it happened to you, Mother—a movement of His new life to you, according to the scriptures and yet beyond, in a way beyond telling.

Meanwhile, Mother, I sense a certain flaming desire in my heart with beautiful thoughts. "How glorious and delightful it would be to see the longed-for face of the Lord, beautiful in form before all the sons of men, no longer abject and vile, no longer having the appearance with which His mother clothed Him, but robed in the garment of immortality and crowned with the diadem with which His Father crowned Him on the day of His resurrection and glory, the day which the Lord has made."[317]

During the day

Lord Jesus, how wonderful to realize more and more that, however blessed and privileged were the women and men disciples to behold You in Your risen glory, we are not less privileged really than they!

When the apostles told Thomas about their experience of You as risen, they were surely not showing off their privilege nor boasting about it. They were surely sharing their experience with the obvious intention of communicating to him the same experience and drawing him into their own experience of You and Your joy.

No wonder then that the part of the initial *kerygma* was the narration, or rather the mere enumeration of Your first appearances: once raised to life on the third day, You appeared first to Cephas and secondly to the Twelve, next to more than five hundred of the brothers and sisters at the same time, then to James, then again to all the apostles, and last of all to Paul too. Lord, to be fair, I'd like to include in this sacred list Your first appearances to Your Mother and to Your other Marys and Your other women disciples. Were not the latter the first to speak of Your appearance as such, heralding every later appearance of Yours?

Lord, is not mere hearing the story of an appearance of Yours experiencing it myself? Anyway, stories in Your Jewish tradition gained their enduring currency partly at least for this very reason; didn't they?

So, Lord, I believe every manifestation of Your risen glory becomes a divine sign. Once it is posited, it is posited once and for all and addressed not only to those immediately intended beneficiaries, but also to all who will be able to contemplate it and welcome its mystery of risen joy, divine joy. Lord, when You appear to anyone in any circumstances—in and through and beyond any concrete advantage bestowed on those immediately concerned—don't You first and foremost manifest (the economy of) salvation in the love of the Father which saves everyone from death to life?

And so, Lord, I believe every contemplation of an apparition of Yours takes us back to the one eternal Resurrection. I take it as a visit from You Yourself, my risen Lord who is forever alive henceforth.[318]

Abba Father, Your act of raising Your Son from the grave ... from the dead, proves something we hardly dream of. The questions we raise seeing Your abandonment of Your Son on the cross are more than answered by the Resurrection. You are no God of misery and You cause no misery. Rather You commiserate the miserable and You wipe the misery with Your mercy. And what is more, You transform it by Your glorious, if unsuspected, alchemy!

And so, in like manner, Your Son surprises His disciples with his unexpected visit to them; He frees them from fear; He removes their doubt; He lifts up their drooping spirit: He breathes forth the Spirit to His men disciples explicitly.

And no less to Your beloved women disciples, though inexplicitly. How they evinced the gifts of Your Spirit and mission right from the time they were surprised by Your unsuspected mode of living, living on a higher level of being, risen being.

May I live with the gifts of the Resurrection always, even at fearful, death-like moments: "Give me, good Lord, an humble, lowly, quiet, peaceable, patient, charitable, kind, tender, and pitiful mind with all my works, and all my words, and all my thoughts, to have a taste of Thy holy, blessed Spirit."[319]

At night

"I'm the Resurrection!" That is what You said, Lord, long before the resurrection! When nobody made sense of Your words, or even could, though they did when they saw You as risen Lord! In Your resurrection appearances to Your beloved You surprised them with the truth of Your resurrection. What they had heard about and did not understand they were beginning to have an inkling of! Lord, may I have an inkling of what I have believed in without, however, understanding it! May I understand it, Lord, in the way and measure You want me to understand ... give me to understand with a heart of faith ... that intuits Your difference in Your appearance ... wearing what else but the mien of the Holy Spirit in Your resurrection.[320]

Like Mary, Your Mother, to start with. She, and none else, had to see You first in Your risen life! If earlier You had had to appear before others like Pilate, Herod, the chief priests and others like a criminal that You were not, now the story is altogether different. Now vindicated and victorious and suffused in glory that is Yours before whom had You to appear first but the one who bore You? She had stood by You, always wanting to understand Your ways: she had to be surprised first by Your vision ... by the revelation of the meaning of all that happened to You earlier. She received from You the supreme significance of Your resurrection, the end stage of the course of Your life from beginning to end. As You were clothed with the glory of grace by Your Abba, You let it fall on Your mother too and draped her with it! And so we pray to her, even as You cannot keep her far from You. The heavenly moment of Your appearance in glory before Your Abba corresponds to the earthly moment of Your appearance to Your *Imma*.

Being the first one to enjoy the presence of your risen Son, Mother Mary, you would share with us what you have received from Him and from the Father and the Spirit. You share with us by your very turning to Him, your admitting us into your company, leading us to Him, and praying to Him with us. Our praying to you now is something called for by your privileged experience of your risen Son. Like Him you have reached the end, even if not the very final end. From this end-experience of yours we want to have the beginning of an experience! An experience that succeeds the Passion and yet flows out of the Passion ... without any break ... constituting the new paradigm of life. Such an experience, Mother, can be nothing but pure, unimaginable grace of your Son. Nothing is here for tears, nothing much less to wail ... All is best![321] Yes, for those certainly who, like you, have first had the courteous love and virtue to mourn enough and aright. And, surprisingly, even for those, like the Emmaus-bound disciples, who cry awry and overmuch.

Lord Jesus, how am I to serve the exercitants at this stage except by rejoicing over what You would be doing in them and to them ... and by thanking You for their grace ... all the while hopefully experiencing more than before what You would bless me with, in this interlinked and irreducible mystery of shame and fame, agony and ecstasy, death and life? In Your sorrow turning to joy may ours too turn so, just as You assured Your disciples in deed and in word (Mt 17:1-8; Jn 16:21-22). In this hope we wait for the glimpse of the glory that is Yours in the resurrection so that we may find ourselves where You are ... even in glory! Graced once with a sense of Your resurrection we shall never miss it; for we shall come to recognize it as a recurring miracle, an ongoing miracle, indeed the unending miracle!

Isn't it the day the Lord has made ... a day whose mysterious beginning we can hardly imagine ... a day that knows no end? Risen Lord, would You not prepare a place in our hearts and minds for the light of this endless day? "Grant that we may have within us this light, the life of the resurrection, and that nothing may take away our delight in You."[322]

Good Lord, would You let us endure so much suffering if it were not to prepare us for Your glory? Your Passion and Resurrection together form a story of total emptiness leading to total fullness.

29. THE JOY THAT IS RESURRECTION

I will not leave you orphaned; I am coming to you.
In a little while the world will no longer see Me,
but you will see Me;
because I live, you also will live. (Jn 14:18-19)
I will continue to rejoice,
for I know that through the help of the Spirit of Jesus Christ
this will turn out for my deliverance. (Phil 1:18-19)

"Shalom lekha (Peace to you);
I am Sar Shalom (Prince of Peace)."
"Won't You, Rabbuni, disabuse me
of all my supposed joys this day?
It'll then be an assurance for me
that You will do all You intend for me in Your victorious goodness
for the simple reason of Your joy ineffable.
Only then I'll know joy! Shalom rav."

At dawn

Risen Lord, now that You are risen and appear to us in *an unseen apparition but filled with faith* what can be our way of proceeding at this time of the retreat? Can we be exercitants only carrying on the Exercises as before? "Yes, My beloved, and yet with a difference of pitch! With a certain elevation of spirit let yourself go and be contemplating." Lord, no wonder that now the exercitant can only be described as *"persona que contempla"*—the person who is contemplating (# 228)! And therefore necessarily ecstatic, standing beside oneself! Glorious Jesus, if all along we had every good reason not to forget ourselves as we meditated on sin or contemplated on Your earthly mysteries now there is every reason to forget us, everything of ourselves, all of ourselves going out in contemplation of Your risen existence. Will not, then, all our affections be inspired by You and Your appearance, irrespective of our condition or situation?[323]

There is indeed something more besides! The affections will be intense, expressive of closeness and seeking union. According to Your promise to the disciples at the Last Supper You come back to them now and reveal Yourself to them. You make or, better still, remake friends with them who were unbelievably much lost friends! Lost to You and much more lost to themselves! When You appear in Your resurrection You unite Yourself to them and them to Yourself ... in an unheard-of "friendship" that goes beyond what is normally known as friendship (# 224)![324]

During the day

Lord Jesus, having sought Your company and kept Your company and followed You all this long while, though not without falling and failing, let me now not lose sight of You, my Jesus, in the last lap of Your revelation, so glorious and joyful. As joy is never in our power be Thou "Jesu, joy of man's desiring".[325]

You inspired someone to voice the appealing invitation: "Let us not lose sight of Jesus, who leads us in our faith and brings it to perfection"—perfection of the joy with which You have taken Your rightful place beside Your Abba Father, bestowed of course by Him (Heb 12:2).

What is this joy, my Lord, the resurrection joy? Is it not simply the transparency and radiance of the Word made flesh wholly turned to God ... and so fully shining in God's pure transparency? Your resurrection and the joy of it—it is "the infinite possibility of the divine life offered to a humanity again made capable of receiving the gift of God."[326] Or better still, it is the actualization of that possibility ... the first actualization opening to our own!

Lord, You had issued Your summons to all, declaring Your manifesto of conquering Your enemies and so entering into Your Abba's glory. Your conquest is not a matter of vindictive destruction and ban and humiliation as of old. It was winning Your human opponents to Your side, and uniting them with You, and leading them to enter the very glory of Abba. And the glory of Abba God itself is nothing but humanity made fully alive with all individual humans fully alive and so become as children of His whom He loves and who therefore love Him in return! So that is Your conquest, Your glory, Your joy! It is the birth of the new Adam (Eph 2:15), new Man or Woman, yes real human, the beginnings of the new creation!

You are the image of the unseen God and the first born of all creation. As You are the Beginning, You were first to be born from the dead ... because God wanted all perfection to be found in You (Col 1:15-16, 18-19)—You, the Word made flesh, and so assuming us in our flesh and thus bringing everything together in Yourself (Eph 3:10), and so taking us into Yourself (Eph 5:27) to become part of Your fullness (Eph 1:23), and so enabling us mature fully with the fullness of Yourself (Eph 4:13).

Lord Jesus, I used to ask for the grace of rejoicing with You in Your great joy, without any consideration of what benefits accrue to us from Your resurrection. I used to think this grace of unconditional joy was the great grace of Your work, though I can't claim I have enjoyed its reception for certain. Today, however, You spring a further surprise revelation. Yes, what a surprise to realize Your great joy of the resurrection is not only what we rightly call Your personal, individual exhilaration and exultation of Your faithfulness to Abba till the last breath, it is sweeping us along with You in Your glorious appearance before Abba. After all, Your Father, as it strikes me, always manifested Himself through You, Jesus, as one always acting in favour of us humans and calling us, together with the whole creation, to enter into His glory.[327] How can it be otherwise in this climactic mystery of resurrection?

190

At night

In our love, knowingly or not we want to know You according to the flesh, and perhaps only in that manner, even as Your disciples did for long. In so far as it is a natural, innocent longing You must provide for its satisfaction; won't You, Lord? That is part of our faith, perhaps naïve and infantile faith, which You in Your love won't disdain even as You make us outgrow it in time.

Anyway You tell us no story of the actual event of Your resurrection but quite something about Your new life and continued living and loving. Yes, what is most surprising is the power of Your ongoing love that draws You, the only Begotten, to Your Abba and simultaneously to us born of Him, begotten by Him. And so our life too becomes a discovery and exercise of interpersonal union with You, Your Father as well as ours, and Your Spirit and ours.[328]

So it is expedient for us, as for the first disciples, that You made Your disappearance from the human scene. The shape of Your manhood You withdrew from our eyes of flesh; only then the love of Your divinity can fasten in our spiritual eyes.[329]

And so we learn also a piece of wisdom. Your Abba God gave You victory after Your hard struggle, indeed in Your very endurance of it. Whatever does God teach us from this? This too perhaps: wisdom is the greatest power of all (Wis 2:12-22; 10:12). So You could ask: "Is it not necessary that the Son of Man should suffer and enter into His glory?" Not to know it is folly; knowing it is wisdom.

30. RESURRECTION AND
CONTEMPLATION TO OBTAINING LOVE

While in their joy the disciples were
disbelieving and still wondering,
Jesus said to them, 'Have you anything here to eat?' (Lk 24:41)
Jesus breathed on the disciples and said:
"Receive the Holy Spirit.
If you forgive the sins of any, they are forgiven. (Jn 20:22-23)

"Do not be afraid, My little soul,
I am the first and the last, and the living one.
I was dead, and see, I am alive for ever and ever."
"With Your surprise victory of love that Your Resurrection is
don't You, Rabbuni, have a surprise for me,
so awesome and yet hopeful?
Won't You let Yourself be surprised because of me too?
It'll be an assurance for me
that I will do all You want from me in Your goodness
for the simple reason that it is no longer beyond me!"

At dawn

Risen Jesus, not having had the privilege of many a Mary or John
I sought to content myself with Your call to believe through
Thomas, our happy twin in faith, and thus to move toward a more
complete faith hankering for no spiritual fireworks of any sort.
Then it was that Thomas along with others assured me that You
have come to me too, and then gone, just as to them. Then it struck
me suddenly that believing in Your resurrection is indeed a means
of entering into its mystery![330] There is indeed no other way of
coming to know it!

As I wondered about its charming truth a later witness shared and shed his light: "I know (Him) because He is living and active. As soon as He arrives within He shakes my sleepy soul into life. He moves and softens and pierces my heart which had been previously hard, stony and twisted out of shape.... He waters the soil and enlightens the gloom; He opens up what was closed and inflames what was frigid. At the same time He makes the twisted roads straight and the rough pathways smooth. And all this done so that my soul may bless the Lord."[331]

I wonder if this is another way of reiterating Your last beatitude occasioned by the unbelief of Thomas. More blessed than those who see and believe are those who do not see but believe, those who in their blind seeing[332] end up happily believing, those whose knowing trust enables them to see even in their blindness; because the blind spot of faith is somehow illuminative.

Anyway, this leads me to think of my role in causing faith in others, especially the exercitants. I learn that, for all the importance of Your apparitions to excite faith in the resurrection, it is the proclamation of it, the gospel, the Word of God, that will prove to be the real and adequate motive of faith.[333] May I open myself to such faith and help my exercitants in doing so themselves. So I don't ask You that I see and touch You. But I do ask that I sense Your touch ... and realize that You are more real than anything I've ever touched and enjoyed!

"Yes, My beloved, My resurrection must become an underlying happiness in you, indeed in every believer and follower. You'll sense it goes deeper than any surface fears."

And so, glorious Jesus, I'll learn to prattle: "My Redeemer lives and so I live! So all shall be well in the end! And what is more, if all shall be well in the end, then in some mysterious manner all is well even right now and will always be, despite the doubts I've to live with in the meantime."[334]

"Well said, My rising beloved, you'll learn a new absorption and so be absorbed in Me, the risen One! You'll forget all of your own life, knowing joy in none else as in Me, raised by Abba God glorious and exulting. What is more, you'll find all your loves and joys in Me, who loved unto the end and beyond to be inundated with the God of joy!"

Even as I am uplifted by this Your outpouring of Your blessing, I feel, gracious Lord, more humbled than elevated especially as a man like St Thomas More prayed so humbly despite his great love for You before he laid down his life for You. May I, then, pray after him thus, in accents that are so Ignatian? Knowing my love for You being never so great, still bear me, good Lord, Thy love and favour, which my love could not, but of Thy great goodness, deserve.[335]

During the day

Dear Jesus, risen from the dead I like to pray, not for an appearance of You to me, but for simply and deeply knowing You are alive and active, energizing all, even me and the exercitants. Your loving women disciples stumble upon the mystery of Your resurrection; You surprised them appearing to them alive and granted them, through and beyond their fear, an inkling of the mystery. And the most important thing is that it is through them that You have the resurrection proclaimed so that, through them, others too may be prepared to receive the mystery. Though I am not ignorant of the resurrection I wonder if I have received the message of the mystery! I don't know the resurrection as I know my fears, failures, foolishness, etc.! Lord, when will You rise in me?

Lord, is there not a significance in the fact that whenever You appeared to anyone You were sure to disappear. In fact, You remained long enough only to lead the chosen ones to recognize You; and once they recognized You, You vanished into thin air. Or, did You vanish into them? Anyhow, it is not a little surprising that no one doubted Your presence after Your disappearance, even if some of them did during the appearance. They were persuaded You were alive; and they could not contain themselves till they could talk about it among themselves, and later tell others about it. You communicated this experience to Your beloved not in any so called privileged place, but here, there and anywhere! This encounter of Your presence was such that, even in Your obvious absence in the usual world of ours, they felt the accompaniment or company or intrusion of Your presence everywhere in any surroundings, in every situation and in every encounter.

Lord, may I have this grace of Your presence, of sensing Your presence, of recognizing Your presence in Your absence, yes, Your presence in Your disguise of a gardener, of a surprise visitor or an unexpected guest, of a co-traveller, of an unsuspected companion, of anyone and everyone, either on the sea shore, or on a long journey or in the very dwelling of mine, or on my way home from some business or near a grave or anywhere and everywhere. By Your incarnation You could not be so, and were not so, before Your resurrection. You were in one place and not another. While You were with one person You were not with another. But in Your state of resurrection You are not time-bound or space-bound or person-bound. Surely one of the true and most sacred effects of the resurrection (# 223.1), bringing home to us the ubiquity of Your Father and Spirit (Ps 139).

So, Lord, You should be there wherever I am, wherever I go, wherever I flee, wherever I search, whenever I am lost, whenever I cry, wherever I am huddled with others out of fear, wherever I hide myself, etc. And so let me recognize You there, and contemplate You there, and know love in all its variety, in all its sensitivity, in all its creativity, yes in all its fun and play, in all its inviting challenge, yes even in its silence, in its struggle, in its sweet commission, in its persuasion, in its ascension, in its surrender, in its past, in its future, in its memory, in its dream and delight, in its undying power, in its permanence, in its gift and task, in its sameness and unique newness.

This will be a particular blessing of Your act of redeeming love leading me to contemplate how much more You'd love to give Yourself to me (# 234.1-2).

After all, I need love wherever I am and look for it and long for it. So Lord, may I know You are alive in love, as indeed You are in Your resurrection. This will be my contemplation for loving, *contemplatio ad amorem.*

You gave a revelation to Hildegard of Bingen which she expressed with others thus: "God hugs you. You are encircled by the arms of the mystery of God."[336] May I enjoy this encircling and enfolding of the arms of God as I contemplate the mystery of Your risen life, of Your cosmic presence in love radiating from Your redeeming resurrection.

In the same spirit I'm moved to say, "Every presence makes me feel that You are near me; every touch is the touch of Your hand; every necessity transmits to me a pulsation of Your will. And so true is this that everything around me that is essential and enduring has become the dominance and, in some way, the substance of Your Heart: Jesus!"[337]

Lord of today, the more You grant me to experience such a grace the more I shall become myself, deeply human, as You intended ... and the more trained I shall be to attain the end for which I was created ... and that, not only in Heaven but also all the way to Heaven, here and now.

At night

On this day of joy I recall this sudden light from Your light: "Becoming joyful means finding ourselves within that whole story (of Your life) which goes from birth to death to resurrection. We belong inside this story for it is our own and it carries us through confusion and suffering and death towards the resurrection."[338]

Having passed so many days and hours with You, dear Jesus, whatever has happened to us in our personal, spiritual being? Have we become familiar enough with You to recognize You in all things and beings and persons always and everywhere ... and so to sense Your hidden manifestations ... and so to be accustomed to Your ubiquity and activity? You know it, Lord, with Your piercing sight and penetrating presence and perpetual dynamic, all suffused in Your kind of love.

Anyway, Lord, risen and pervasive, I have over the years stumbled upon a certain contemplation of You ... momentarily ... which I long to have constantly. Behind and beyond contemplating Your presence and dynamism outside me I'd contemplate You inside me ... not in quiet meditation but in engrossing action. I'd like to sense You and be in actual touch with You while walking, seeing, tasting, hearing and whatever else I may be doing. Then hopefully I'll find You even in my very act of interior thinking or exterior speaking.[339] I'm able to contemplate thus negatively, because when I'm unable to do any of this I call You for help. But when I'm able because of Your power flowing into me, somehow I fail to be aware of You; and fail to be sensitive enough to contemplate You positively.

Just as I can call all creatures so that they may assist me in praising God so may I call all the parts of myself with all their regular, active powers to this one life task of praise!

Lord of all creatures, how close this experience is to where we started with the *Fundamentum*! And yet how far! One is contained in the other. We began, Lord, with a dose of common sense: "common sense" of the created universe. We end up, Lord, with an "uncommon sense" of the same. Have we really grown to see and view and appreciate reality as it is in itself, in its very transparency of littleness in itself and greatness in God? In my own littleness, then, I shall testify to the light of the glory of God and experience greatness.

If in the beginning we had failed, as creatures, to realize the joyous duty of praise, reverence and service of God, now we would see the foolishness of it, Lord God. Power alone would never make You God. You are no proud sovereign but the divine server and servant in love and humility of Your creation. What makes You God and demands our adoration is that You went out of Yourself in creation, and shared the gift of being with Your creatures. You have continued to go forth from Yourself through evolutionary history and human history. In Jesus Christ, we believe, You came forth from Your transcendence in a new and decisive way, the unsurpassable and irrevocable way of ultimate immanence and mutual indwelling. In the Spirit, You still come forth to us and draw us into the life of the Spirit.

And so I make bold to pray in mystic style for Your secret, Your secret of joy, that some like G. K. Chesterton intuited. You, Lord, are all joy, overflowing mirth, infinite rapture. You'll extend it, won't You, even into me, into my whole being? Yes, even into my body, so that my face and my heart and my mouth and all my limbs and members feel Your joy. I dream of the day when I can say as some have said: "the sea is not so full of water as I am of joy."[340]

"And I want you to know it even in your suffering and passion. You certainly don't suspect anything of joy in My Passion. But if you let My words make home in you it will dawn on you that at the very onset of My Passion I chose joy that made Me assure My disciples of peace, courage, love, yes, joy too (Jn 14:27-28; 15:11-12; 16:6-7, 20-22). I was right in the thick of disloyalty or cowardice or betrayal or hatred; but I chose Abba God and with Him all joy. Choosing hidden joy, joy in or in spite of human evil is joy itself! After all, joy like love is stronger than death! Joy is sensible enough not to deny distress or death but fertilizes it all for more joy."[341]

Risen Lord, let us hitch a ride with You as You joyously appear and disappear and move among us and stir us from wherever we are.

"Perhaps, now you may understand the uncommon depiction of Me smiling on the cross or revelation of Me laughing merrily away at My last breath."[342]

31. *CONTEMPLATIO AD AMOREM*

Do you not know that you are God's temple
and that God's Spirit dwells in you? (1 Cor 3:16)
The spirit of the Lord has filled the world,
and that which holds all things together
knows what is said. (Wis 1:7)

"Now is the fullness of time to gather up all things in Me,
things in heaven and things on earth,
according to the good pleasure of Abba Father
made known in His Son."
"This day, Rabbuni, please, grant me the favour
to ask You nothing whatever.
It'll be an assurance for me
that You have given me everything that I could possibly want!
Meanwhile I wait for Your love and grace
for the simple reason that You know better than I!"

At dawn

Abba Father, You love us and contemplate us. That was so right
from the beginning of creation. And so You pronounced every bit
of creation good, all blessed ... You even rested and rejoiced in
them ... especially in Your image and likeness borne by humanity.
May we follow suit ... desire to ... learn to contemplate You ... in
Your creation ... and above Your creation... without tiring.

Even when the best of Your creation became the worst and was
lost You searched with Your resounding voice, "Where are you?"
And You never gave up on it abandoning it for good. For You were
the One who taught Your children to walk; You took them in Your

arms, drew them to Yourself with tenderness, bent down to them and fed them (Hos 11:3-4).

And so now we want to seek Your presence, to recognize Your face, to hear Your word, to sense Your touch, etc., in all that You have filled us with and surrounded us with. May we know to contemplate Your goodness and love in matter, in organism, in living being, in human being ... and indeed human beings of all sorts—yes, in cosmos inner as well as outer. That will be a new sighting of the burning bush within ourselves and between us and what surrounds us.[343] Then we will know ... what it is to love You ... and, more than that, to be loved by You. And that will be creation once again in our level, imitating what happened at Your level in the beginning! In this new beginning which we experience here and now, Your eternal Presence becomes intimate and continual, generating within us a love that is overflowing as well as exclusive.[344] Apart from the surd of sin how full the universe is with God.[345]

During the day

Lord, wherever are You? Far and yet near? Wherever am I? Yes, far and yet near?

In the space-time of action that I call prayer You are there! Near though far! And I? I too am there, though, only more or less! More far than near. Or even, perhaps, never near and always far!

In the space-time of all that is not prayer, Lord, I am everywhere and You are nowhere! That would *seem* to be the objective reality! Anyway, that is the psychological reality of subjective experience ... of myself as well as of others.

I am on the earth, of the earth, surrounded by earthly things or earthlings like or unlike myself! I am always in their midst, seeing them or holding them or handling them or using them or throwing them or consuming them or keeping them safe, etc. I am conscious of their closeness either pleasant or painful, attractive or repulsive, life-giving or death-dealing, etc. So living, I may look for You when things don't go well, yes, may look for You whom I didn't seem to need till then.

If only, Lord, I could do all this somewhat differently: meaningfully, curiously, questioningly, thoughtfully, intuitively, contemplatively! What shall I find? Is there a chance of finding some reality? Anyone who searches will surely find! What will it be? If one can say what it is, there is no need of searching! As I search am I equal to the task: being eager, sensitive, delicate, persevering, vigilant, etc.? If I don't prove myself unequal to the task, Lord, that itself would be no small grace!

Since I believe You are the Creator can I, may I, find You there creating, loving, yes creatively loving? Are You not constantly creating what You once loved and created, and have not ceased doing so, Creator Lord of love? In so lovingly creating constantly are You not there sustaining every creature: me and everyone and everything around me? So, then, let me see, perceive, understand and wonder at whatever You are pleased to reveal to me in my searching attempt! Is it not "listening to the truth of things"?[346] Let me enjoy this bit of holy curiosity, quite close to courtesy as well as creativity?

I pray with one of Your enlightened ones: "Lord, grant that I may see, that I may see You, that I may see and feel You present in all things and animating all things."[347] Or again, with another of Your beloved souls I'd like to say: "I see Him who is being, and I see how He is the being of all creatures,"[348] and how every creature is filled with Him by His eternal embrace of love!

"My beloved, did you ever wonder I should be more familiar to you than your nearest neighbour? When you so wonder I'll touch your heart and it shall know that the only knowledge it can have is of Me!"[349]

Such being reality ... reality of You, I love to rehearse Your unsuspected revelation: "Oh! The love of the Lord is the essence of all that I've here on earth!"

"All things which are not God are grasped, each in its inmost being, as something transparent, through which God shines forth. God, who has veiled Himself in His creatures, can be found only if this veil is lifted from them. For in Christ Jesus, the creator became a creature"[350] of love and so loving. Eternity has entered time! And so if, earlier, time and things temporal often came between us and our future, in Christ time becomes transparent to eternity[351] and everything in time a mirror of eternal values! So there is a new openness to all creation and to You, the Creator and Redeemer and Sanctifier. If there was a time of keeping our distance from certain human experiences You have now brought us to the time when we can immerse ourselves in the enjoyment of everything! Isn't it thus a matter of finding You in everything and *vice versa*, and that everywhere, and always? How true it is, then, that creation is a sacrament of God![352] And so I like the gem of an idea that at the final judgment the only question You would ask is whether we enjoyed Your creation![353]

Are we sure of having found You, God of love, except when You put Yourself at our disposal because we ourselves are—seek to be—entirely Yours?[354] As You taught, many an ancient Indian *sannyasi* have listed in a *subhashita* the graded moments and movements of love: "one gives and receives; tells secrets and asks; enjoys and causes enjoyment."[355]

And today, triune God, I thought I was a privy to a wonderful conversation of You Three with a fourth one! I heard first Papa God speak to me:

"Honey, I've never placed an expectation on you or anyone else. The idea behind expectations requires that someone does not know the future or outcome and is trying to control behaviour to get the desired result.... I know you and everything about you.... What I do have is a constant and living expectancy in our relationship, and I give you an ability to respond to any situation and circumstance in which you find yourself. To the degree that you resort to expectations and responsibilities, to that degree you neither know Me nor trust Me."

"And," added (You,) Jesus, "to that degree you'll live in fear."

Papa again (joined): "You see ... I don't just want a piece of you and a piece of your life.... I want all of you and all of every part of you and your day."

(And You,) Jesus now spoke again: "I don't want to be first among a list of values; I want to be at the centre of everything. When I live in you, then together we can live through everything that happens to you. Rather than the top of a pyramid, I want to be the centre of a mobile, where everything in your life—your friends, family, occupation, thoughts, activities—is connected to Me but moves with the wind, in and out and back and forth, in an incredible dance of being."

"And I," concluded (the Spirit), "am the wind!"[356]

What could I do but shudder and surrender only to be embraced and raised to know myself smiling for the first time!

At night

Risen Jesus, You are Lord of day and of night. We are so much creatures of the day and so trying to change even the night into day. Today I like to think that even night can be in Your light as You are the Lord of night too. You have redeemed all the days as You kept us turned to You in prayer. Tonight as I contemplate You I dream of finding You in the darkness of the night, in the quiet of the night, in the rest from labour, in our doing nothing conscious so that You will do in us what You choose in our unconscious as we make of our very sleep a religious act of contemplative surrender to Your abiding presence and providence!

"My beloved, I love what you say! You've spoken more truly than you realize! You know why I was born? The ultimate reason was to give life to all. If I taught or showed the way or set an example to follow in life and death it was finally that you may have life and all may have it abundantly. And you'll have life only if you let Me abide in you; yes, if I abide in you and make you abide in Me! Apart from My life inside you, you can't be living or doing anything good! So, My beloved, find the resurrection in yourself because of Me!"

Feeling wonderful I pray, Abba, with Your beloved ones: "We must praise Thy goodness that Thou hast left nothing undone to draw us to Thyself." I feel uncomfortable, though, to add with others, "But one thing we ask of Thee, our God, not to cease Thy work in our improvement." However I like to continue with them, "Let us tend towards Thee, no matter by what means, and be fruitful in good works, for the sake of Jesus Christ our Lord. Amen."[357] And what is more, I am hoping to say in time—in Your time—with our new Jesuit Beatus Bernardo de Hoyos: "I see everything in my heart moving towards God, drawn like iron to a magnet. It desires only God, searches only for God, and longs only for God."[358] As indeed all saints learnt sooner or later to say the same, each in his or her way; like Saint Jeanne Jugan, for example, who could say, "In the background of every least event, in filigree behind creatures, God stands. As for me, I no longer see anything but God."[359]

Thus Your love cannot but unveil its secret, great secret: "which transforms our action into contemplation, and shows forth in everyone of our actions the radiance of an unceasing Presence. The continuity of a dialogue that neither persons, nor events have power to interrupt.... Could we still speak of anything merely of this world in (our) life, of common tasks, or lowly? When, with

205

so much ease, You stamp the divine on human actions and vice versa?"[360]

With all this, what greater fruitfulness can there be than being ourselves a gift to others as every bit of creation has been a gift to us and, above all, God's own self (## 234:1-2; 237:1).

But, knowing my love for You being never so great (even as Thomas More prayed despite his great love for You before he laid down his life for You) I pray after him: "(Still) bear me, good Lord, Thy love and favour, which my love could not, but of Thy great goodness, deserve".[361] Thy love, that Dante found along with the Psalmists of old, that moves the sun and the other stars.[362]

APPENDIX

1. Facing the bugaboo of long retreat

Lord ever different, every long retreat is different, but not in the way You are, Lord, as I was rudely surprised to learn in the last retreat. Different in the kind of difficult persons that the retreatants seem to me or turn out to be for me. This is certainly not to deny that there were also balancing surprises of candour, confidence and wonderful response, along with certain opportunities of close relationship. I'm afraid, however, that I am more affected by the rude surprises than pleasant ones! So I am at times beset by a sense of inability or ineptitude; at other times haunted by a mood of uselessness or even dread.

Amidst such varying disturbances of the dark gloom, lead, kindly Light. In Your light let me see light. If, as I believe, You shine there in any situation, You are not any less shining in the situation of the unfolding of the retreat and retreatants. As You let Your light dawn on me in this unknown, somewhat disturbing situation, may I awaken to Your unique presence above all other presences, Your unconditional, uncompromising presence as the all-knowing Director. Such being the fact, Lord, I ought not, dare not, assume the over-all responsibility for the retreat. I am—can be—only a helper, a helper giving some visibility to You and Your help. Disowning any more responsibility than this their due, I want to withdraw to my own place as "the giver of the Exercises", an awkward expression that however reveals better my right position in relation to You, the Sole Director by right.

Yes, Lord, the truth is that You are the Director. With You, therefore, lies the whole responsibility of making the retreat a success, a real, not apparent, success. You start to work with the exercitants long before I even come into the picture. When I come into contact with them I'd insist, therefore, from start to finish, one basic gospel experience ... permeating the Exercises though not found explicitly in it. The experience is of You ... as the One who is at work in us, enabling us both to will and to work for Your good pleasure (Ph 2:13). It is of You as the power at work with us, able to accomplish abundantly far more than all we can ask or imagine (Eph 3:20). We exist in no other way at any time, even outside the retreat time, apart from You.

During the retreat this reality of You working in us is, if anything, all the more true and hopefully manifest too! Because during the retreat we seem to meet with disturbing, disabling, destructive powers. The retreat of the Exercises is no smooth enterprise involving me and You. Powers of evil more than equal to my powers emerge quietly. They may be even difficult to detect. They may be also tantalizing. It is especially then, Lord, I'll remind myself and the exercitants that there is one far, far, infinitely far above me ... and yet invariably at work in us so that we will all succeed ... in an astonishing manner. So then I do not say that the burden of success rests with You; rather I believe it is a matter of course with You!

Of course, I fail to advert to all this always. Then I tend to fear that not much good will happen in the Exercises and that I cannot do anything to change the course for the better. But when I adhere to the truth of You as the Director of us all I sense bright prospects ... like someone scattering seeds in his field and going about his daily business without fuss even in the face of difficulties, only to find in due course of time the harvest ready (Mt 13:3-9; Mk 4:26-29).

Once I'm so carried away by this assured success-to-be, a fear with a difference comes over me; a "holy fear" on the "holy ground" of the retreat. Where You keep coming and going I dare not tread there, for fear that, in my inadequacy I may get in Your way or even mess up things in my stupid fervour.

At the same time, I know moments when I knew I was far from discerning about myself and my ways during the retreat; and yet, in my shame, I trusted in Your continued good work uncompromised by anything of my unworthiness and conditioned only by Your sovereignty. I am grateful to You for it, Lord. Though I wouldn't like to repeat the earlier falls, they have taught me my status as only a giver of the Exercises. Director Lord, ever directing us, I, being no more than a giver—a passer—I feel even in my dark defeat: "I am free enough to undertake the work ... no matter how aware I am of vast gaps in my inner life and my spiritual experience. I may very well be shown up as one who is indeed very poor in spirit; but does this matter, since the start, the pace and the goal of the retreat are set, not by me, but by God?... But however poorly I am responding to God's calls in my own life, I can at least present Christ and the Saints to retreatants, accompany them on their journey, support them and help them reflect on what is happening in their encounter with God, and hold them at those critical junctures where they see clearly what God wants, but experience the temptation to evade the issue and to move to something else. And so, though I may be far from the goal myself, I know the way, and so can help others find it."[363]

Somehow, I don't fear about the success of the retreat in the beginning, but only when I find some difficulties or conflicts cropping up in the course of the retreat. At least in three retreats I have had sleepless nights because of the behaviour of one or two retreatants. In such moments especially when I am all but lost, burst upon my scene of woe with the authority that is Yours as all-knowing Director. Then, Lord, I won't lose Your saving Direction to me or within me, meant either for myself or the retreatants.

And so, Christ Jesus, even if our faith is very little, we want to listen to you when you say to us: turn towards Abba God and put your trust in His kingdom (Mt 6:33).

2. Quies Day

Papa God, on this day of rest,
won't You help us to ask nothing
but (learn to) receive everything from You?
It'll be an assurance for us
that we will do what we can't do
and be what we can't be
by ourselves!

Today we'll surely see ourselves in our all too human weakness and so all the more we want to see You in all Your power that is love! And so I feel thrilled to lisp: "Grant, O Lord God, that we may cleave to thee without parting, worship thee without wearying, serve thee without failing, faithfully seek thee, happily find thee, for ever possess thee, the one only God blessed world without end, Amen."[364]

3. Primary words

"No matter what they speak of they always whisper something about everything. If one tries to pace out their boundary, one always becomes lost in the infinite....

"There is a knowledge which stands before the mystery of unity in multiplicity... This knowledge makes use of primordial words, which evoke the mystery. It is like always indistinct and obscure, like the reality itself which by means of such words of knowledge obtains possession of us and draws us into its unsounded depths. In the primordial words spirit and flesh, the signified and its symbol ... are still freshly and originally one—which does not mean, simply the same.... "O star and flower, spirit and garment, love, sorrow and time and eternity!" exclaims Brentano, the Catholic poet.... Can one say what it means? Or is it not precisely an uttering of primordial words, which one must understand without having to explain them by means of "clearer" and cheaper words?.... They are deeper and truer than the worn-down verbal coins of daily intellectual intercourse which one often likes to call "clear ideas" because habit dispenses one from thinking anything at all in their use.

"In every primordial word there is signified a piece of reality in which a door is mysteriously opened for us into the unfathomable depths of true reality in general. The transition from the individual to the infinite in infinite movement, which is called by thinkers the transcendence of the spirit, itself belong to the content of the primordial word. That is why it is more than a mere word: it is the soft music of the infinite movement of the spirit and of love for God, which begins with some small thing of this earth, which is seemingly the only thing meant by this word."[365]

In the Spiritual Exercises the first primordial word is "man" in Principle and Foundation, which contains others God, soul, creatures, then later sin, self, pain, death, hurt, humiliation, humility, Christ, passion, resurrection, etc!

4. Repetition

Lord, I'm ashamed to confess that I can feel bored with You! I don't bother whether I give You time enough for Your words to reach me beyond the surface. Further I'm not ashamed of missing Your message. I can be tired of hearing Your words, while calculating the time I pass with You.

Would that I could attempt at "burrowing deeper into the truths of salvation" by the simple, natural method of repetition! Perhaps I should learn it from my Mother who, like all mothers, knows the experience of repetition in their life, so much imprinted in their bodies and psyches. "It is a proficiency we can acquire by knowing how to listen to our own inner depth, a wisdom born of fruitful patience and waiting. When we put repetition into practice, following the guidelines suggested by Ignatius, our hearts patiently acquire fresh light and luminosity."[366]

5. At the end

Did we pay heed to where the Spirit has been leading us? Anyway, Lord, now we would like to keep steadily and slowly moving ahead, like Ignatius, "with a wise foolishness (*sapienter imprudens*) in the simplicity of a heart"[367] that reposes in You.

"My beloved, what I've imparted to you and affirmed in you and taught you have had their effect, clearly or obscurely, slowly or quickly. However you must know they'll continue to do so in course of time! That is the spirit in which you must learn to appreciate all My works."

Yes, Lord, I was really surprised to learn this: many particular touches of God can come to pass in souls that neither they nor their director can understand until later, at the opportune time.[368]

ENDNOTES

1   See Marti E. Palmer (tr. and ed.), *On Giving the* Spiritual Exercises, *The Early Jesuit Manuscript Directories and the Official Directory of 1599* (St Louis: Institute of Jesuit Sources, 1996), pp. 18-19.

2   See ibid., pp. 109, 110, 799.

3   See ibid., pp. 123-124.

4   See ibid., p. 202.

5   See ibid., p. 243.

6   *Directory to the Spiritual Exercises*, V, 8, in W. H. Longridge (tr. and com.), *The Spiritual Exercises of St Ignatius Loyola* (London: A. R. Mowbray and Co., 1955), p. 287.

7   Ibid., V, 2, p. 286.

8   *Spiritual Exercises and its first Commentaries* in *Monumenta Ignatiana* (MI), series II, tomus 1 (Madrid, 1919), p. 949.

9   Hugo Rahner, *Ignatius the Theologian*, tr. Michael Barry, (London: Geoffrey Chapman, 1968), p. 186 (hereafter H. Rahner, *Ignatius*).

10 See H. Rahner, *Ignatius*, p. 82.

11 See H. Rahner, *Ignatius*, p. 150.

12 Fontes Narrativi de Sancto Ignacio II as in H. Rahner, *Ignatius*, p. 10.

13 See St Ignatius of Loyola, *The Constitutions of the Society of Jesus*, no. 813. See Paul G. Crowely, *Theological Studies* 52 (1991), p. 454, n. 7. Leonard Sweet has claimed that the words came to the Saint in a dream. See his *So Beautiful: Divine Design for Life and the Church* (Colorado Springs, CO: David C. Cook, 2009), p. 23.

14 See Palmer (tr. and ed.), *On Giving the* Spiritual Exercises, p. 54.

15 "The First Week: Practical Questions", in *The Way of Ignatius Loyola*, edited by P. Sheldrake (St Louis, MO: Institute of Jesuit Sources, 1991), p. 53. Hereafter *Way of Ignatius*.

16 "The One Who Gives the Exercises" as in *Way of Ignatius*, p. 181.

17 Thomas A Kempis, *The Imitation of Christ*, Book III, ch. 49.

18 ALL BIBLICAL REFERENCES ARE TO NRSV, unless otherwise mentioned.

19 *Hamlet* V, ii.

20 *Lear* V, ii.

21 St Therese of Lisieux, *St Therese of Lisieux: Her Last Conversations*, tr. J. Clarke (Washington, DC: ICS Publications, 1977), p. 142.

22 As Hugh of St Victor put it.

23 Bernard of Clairvaux, *On the Song of Songs*, in 4 volumes, tr. Kilian Walsh, Irene Edmonds (Kalamazoo, MI: ICS Publications, 1971-1980), vol. I, sermon 17, nos 1-2, pp. 126-127 as in Ralph Martin, *The Fulfilment of All Desire* (Steubenville, Ohio: Emmaus Road, 2006), p. 202.

24 St Ignatius of Loyola, *The Constitutions of the Society of Jesus* (St Louis: Institute of Jesuit Sources, 1970), n. 414.

25 See Brian Grogan in *Way of Ignatius*, pp. 42-48.

26 From the *Directory of 1591*, MI II, 2, p. 682 as cited by H. Rahner, *Ignatius*, p. 140.

27 See the Introduction to the *Directory* in Longridge, *The Spiritual Exercises*, # 8, p. 275.

28 See John J. English, *Spiritual Freedom* (Chicago: Loyola University Press, 1995), p. 199.

29 See the *Directory* in Longridge, *The Spiritual Exercises*, II, 4, p. 280.

30 Such references are to the paragraphs with subsections in George E. Ganss, *The Spiritual Exercises, A Translation and Commentary* (Anand: GSP, 1993).

31 See the *Directory* in Longridge, *The Spiritual Exercises*, V, 1, p. 286.

32 The idea of *helping ourselves* comes out forcefully in Elder Mullan's translation of *The Spiritual Exercises*. See http://sacred-texts.com/chr/seil/seil05.htm

33 See Jean Laplace, *An Experience of Life in the Spirit*, tr. Eugene L. Donahue (Chicago: Franciscan Herald Press, 1977), p. 17.

34 See Osho, *Just Like That*, pp. 4, 9. See www.osho.com/iosho/library/read-book?p...

35 Erich Przywara, *The Divine Majesty*, tr. T. Corbishley (London: Collins, 1971), p. 94.

36 Etty Hillesum, *An Interrupted Life* as in Alexandra Pleshoyano, "Etty Hillesum: For God and With God", *The Way* 44/1 (January 2005), p. 16.

37 St Ignatius' letters begin often with some such expression; see *Letters of St Ignatius of Loyola*, tr. W. J. Young (Chicago: Loyola University Press, 1959), pp. 43, 49 *et passim*.

38 So said some early commentators on the *Exercises* in MI II, 2 (Rome, 1955), p. 242 as in H. Rahner, *Ignatius*, p. 101.

39 *Thesaurus Spiritualis Societatis Jesu*, Santander, 1950, 316 as in Hermann Rodriguez Osorio, "Spiritual Accompaniment during the Spiritual Exercises", *Review of Ignatian Spirituality*, XXXVI, I (2005), n. 108, p. 74.

40 Benjamin Gonzalez Buelta, *En el aliento de Dios, Salmos de Gratitud* as in H. R. Osorio, "Spiritual Accompaniment during the Spiritual Exercises", *Review of Ignatian Spirituality*, XXXVI, I (2005), n. 108, p. 74.

41 James Brodrick, *The Origin of the Jesuits* (London: Longmans, Green & Co., 1940), p. 20.

42 Simon Decloux, "How God Accompanied Ignatius: A Paradigm for us in 'Helping Souls'", *Review of Ignatian Spirituality*, XXXVI, I (2005), n. 108, p. 13.

43 Adapted from an unusual sharing of St Ignatius. See H. Rahner, *Ignatius*, p. 5.

44 A classical proof is Longridge and later the Anglican Society of Retreat Directors, Series *Subsidia ad Exercitia* (CIS), n. 17. See also the witness of the Protestant theologian, Egon W. Gerdes in his Foreword to John F. X. Sheehan, *On Becoming Whole in Christ* (Chicago, Il.: Loyola Univ. Press, 1978), pp. 5-6.

45 K. Rahner, *Ignatius of Loyola* (London: Collins, 1979), p. 11.

46 See St John Climacus, *The Ladder of Divine Ascent* (further details untraceable for me).

47 Jean Laplace, *An Experience of Life in the Spirit*, p. 27.

48 See the Directory dictated to Alonso de Vitorio in Palmer, *On Giving the Spiritual Exercises*, p. 20.

49 See Jean Laplace, *An Experience of Life in the Spirit*, p. 127.

50 J. Corbon, *L'experience chretienne dans la Bible* (Paris, 1963) as in Gilles Cusson, *Biblical Theology and Spiritual Exercises* (St Louis, MO: Institute of Jesuit Sources, 1988), p. 157.

51 See John English, *Spiritual Freedom*, p. 46.

52 As in the tradition of the early Celtic Church. See John O'Donahue, *Anam Cara* (New York: Harper Perennial, 1998), pp. 13-17.

53 See Directoria Exercitiorum Spiritualium (1540-1594) in MI, II, II (Romae, 1955), nn. 95-96 as in William A. M. Peters, *The Spiritual Exercises of St Ignatius. Exposition and Interpretation* (Rome: CIS, 1980), p. 16.

54 Blaise Pascal, *Pensées*, tr. W. F. Trotter (New York: Modern Library, 1941), no. 554.

55 Based on *The Spiritual Canticle*, stanza 10 in *The Collected Works of John of the Cross*, tr. K. Kavanaugh and O. Rodriguez (London: Nelson, 1966), p. 411.

56 Jean Laplace, *An Experience of Life in the Spirit*, p. 46.

57 See Directory of Fr Vitoria, MI II, 2, p. 100 as in H. Rahner, *Ignatius*, p. 129.

58 See Michael Casey, *Toward God* (Liguori, MO: Ligurori/Triumph, 1989), p. 139.

59 Edouard Pousset, *Life in Faith and Freedom* (Anand: Gujarat Sahitya Prakash, 1980), p. 18.

60 The *Exercises of Master John Codure* as in Rogelio Garacia Mateo, *The Way*, 44, n. 1 (Jan. 2005), p. 111.

61 W. H. Longridge, *The Spiritual Exercises of St Ignatius Loyola*, p. 43.

[62] See Timothy P. Muldoon, "Postmodern Spirituality and the Ignatian *Fundamentum*", *The Way*, 44, no. 1 (January 2005), p. 95.

[63] Juan Luis Segundo, *The Christ of the Ignatian Exercises*, tr. John Drury (London: Sheed and Ward, 1988), p. 79.

[64] Segundo, *The Christ of the Ignatian Exercises*, p. 79.

[65] See *The Exercises of Master John* as in Rogelio Garcia Mateo, "The 'accomodated texts' and the interpretation of the *Spiritual Exercises*", *The Way*, 44/1 (January 2005), pp. 110-111.

[66] Jean Laplace, *An Experience of Life in the Spirit*, p. 38.

[67] Based on Bernard, *On the Song of Songs*, vol. iv, sermon 83, nos. 1-2, p. 181 as in Martin, *The Fulfilment of All Desire*, p. 186.

[68] Following Jerome Nadal; see GC 35, Decree 2, n. 14.

[69] See http://www.gutenberg.org/files/48242/48242-8.txt for this prayer of Thomas à Kempis.

[70] See H. G. Wood, *Belief and Unbelief since 1850* (Cambridge University Press, 2014), p. 96.

[71] See H. Rahner, *Ignatius*, pp. 102-103.

[72] See www.luminarium.org/renlit/moredevoutprayer.htm for this devout prayer of St Thomas More after his condemnation to death.

[73] K. Rahner, *Spiritual Exercises*, tr. K. Baker (London & Melbourne: Sheed & Ward, 1997), p. 18.

[74] See *The Documents of Vatican II*, ed. Walter Abbot (New York: America Press, 1966), p. 710.

[75] Like C. G. Jung, who was more interested in the manner and the method than in the matter and the marrow. See his *Dreams* (London: Ark Paperbacks, 1985), p. 201.

[76] Slightly adapted from a letter to Juan Pascual's mother, MI, Epp I, 92 as in Jose Calveras, *The Harvest-Field of the Spiritual Exercises of St Ignatius* (Bombay: St Xaviers, 1949), p. 43.

[77] S. Kierkegaard, as in Ida Coudenhove, "The Nature of Sanctity", in *A Second Sheed and Ward Anthology* (London: Sheed and Ward, 1933), p. 206.

[78] In a letter as in David Lonsdale, "The Serpent's Tail: Rules for Discernment", in *Way of Ignatius*, p. 165.

[79] Egide van Broeckhoven, *A Friend to all Men* (Danville, NJ: Dimension Books, 1977), p. 35.

[80] Egide van Broeckhoven, *A Friend to all Men*, p. 24.

[81] Timothy Radcliffe, *What is the Point of Being Christian?* (London: Burns and Oates, 2006), p. 127.

[82] Egide van Broeckhoven, *A Friend to All Men*, p. 35.

83 From the retreats of Teilhard in 1940 and 1945 as in Henri de Lubac, *The Faith of Teilhard de Chardin* (London: Burns and Oates, 1965), p. 83.

84 As an Orthodox tradition has it. See John Baggley, *Icons* (London: Catholic Truth Society, 2007), p. 88.

85 See the opening verse of *Īśā Upanishad*.

86 See M. Casey, *Toward God*, p. 2.

87 https://www.goodreads.com/author/quotes/24706.John_Henry_Newman (May 28, 2015)

88 See Laplace, *An Experience of Life in the Spirit*, pp. 51-52.

89 Pascal, *Pensées*, no. 798.

90 Laplace, *An Experience of Life in the Spirit*, p. 49.

91 See St Bernard, *Sermons on the Song of Songs* as in M. Casey, *Toward God*, p. 157.

92 See Pascal, *Pensées*, no. 553.

93 See http://www.gutenberg.org/files/1439/1439-h/1439-h.htm for this poem by Olive Schreiner.

94 To Pascal for example; see his *Pensées*, no. 552.

95 Bernard, *On the Song of Songs*, v. III, sermon 54, no. 8, pp. 76-7 as in Martin, *The Fulfillment of All Desire*, p. 167.

96 Pascal, *Pensées*, no. 552.

97 Laplace, *An Experience of Life in the Spirit*, p. 60.

98 M. Casey, *Toward God*, pp. 149-150.

99 Gandhi, *All Men are Brothers* (New York: Continuum, 2005), p. 54.

100 Josef Sellmair, *The Priest in the World*, tr. B. Battershaw (London: Catholic Book Club, 1954), p. 120.

101 See K. Rahner, *Spiritual Exercises*, p. 28.

102 See Henri J. M. Nouwen, *The Return of the Prodigal Son* (London: DLT, 1994), p. 127: "Jesus, the Beloved of the Father, leaves his Father's home to take on the sins of God's wayward children and bring them home. But, while leaving, he stays close to the Father and through total obedience offers healing to his resentful brothers and sisters."

103 Ben Jonson, *A Hymn to God the Father.*

104 As in Pousset, *Life in Faith and Freedom*, p. 49.

105 See Romano Guardini, *Prayers from Theology* (New York: Herder and Herder, 1959), p. 27.

106 See http://www.stjohndc.org/Russian/fathers/FathersE/e_9511b.htm for this saying of St Isaac the Syrian.

107 As in the best of religious traditions: Christian or Buddhist.

[108] Laplace, *An Experience of Life in the Spirit*, p. 63.

[109] Laplace, *An Experience of Life in the Spirit*, p. 64.

[110] Eric Milner White, "Advent", *My God, My Glory* (Triangle, 1994) as in *Tablet* 28 Dec., 2009, p. 20.

[111] Ben Jonson, *An Hymn to God the Father*.

[112] See www. luminarium. org/renlit/ moredevoutprayer.htm for this devout prayer of St Thomas More.

[113] Pascal, *Pensées*, no. 552.

[114] C. S. Lewis, *Surprised by Joy* (New York: Harcourt, Brace & World: 1955), p. 226.

[115] See John of the Cross, *The Spiritual Canticle*, stanza 28.

[116] See Dag Hammarskjöld, *Markings* (London: Faber and Faber, 1964), p. 99.

[117] Laplace, *An Experience of Life in the Spirit*, p. 58.

[118] K. Rahner, *On Prayer* (Mahwah, NJ: Paulist Press Deus Books, 1968), p. 94.

[119] St Augustine, *Confessions*, tr. Henry Chadwick (Oxford: Oxford Univ. Press, 1991), bk viii, no. 25, p. 150.

[120] H. Rahner, *Ignatius*, p. 87.

[121] H. Rahner, *Ignatius*, p. 86.

[122] As St Gregory the Great wrote in a letter. See George E. Ganss, *The Spiritual Exercises, A Translation and Commentary* (Anand: GSP, 1993), p. 196, n. 161.

[123] As Henri Nowen wrote; see http://www.fumchurst.org/2015-lenten-devotional/

[124] See www. luminarium.org/renlit/moredevoutprayer.htm for this devout prayer of St Thomas More with a slight change.

[125] Pousset, *Life in Faith and Freedom*, p. 50. See also Michael Ivens, *Understanding the Spiritual Exercises* (Herefordshire: Gracewing, 1998), p. 49.

[126] Pousset, *Life in Faith and Freedom*, p. 65.

[127] Pousset, *Life in Faith and Freedom*, p. 50.

[128] See Pascal, *Pensées*, no. 434.

[129] Silvanus of Athos; see Laplace, *An Experience of Life in the Spirit*, p. 62.

[130] Based on Bernard, *On the Song of Songs*, vol. III, ser. 57, nn. 7-8, in Martin, *The Fulfilment of All Desire*, p. 362.

[131] St Thomas Aquinas, *Contra Gentiles*, III 122, as in Joseph Rickaby, *Spiritual Exercises* of *St Ignatius Loyola* (London: Burns & Oates, 1915), p. 36.

[132] Ladislaus Boros, *God is With Us* (London: Burns and Oates, 1967), p. 93; see also pp. 85, 91.

[133] See *Story of a Soul: Autobiography of St Therese of Lisieux*, (Trivandrum: Carmel Publishing House, 1997), p. 83.

[134] See Catherine of Siena, tr. & intro. Suzanne Noffke, *The Dialogue* (The Classics of Western Spirituality, New York/Mahwah, NJ: 1980) ch. 66, p. 124. See also H. Rahner, *Ignatius*, 86.

[135] Pascal, *Pensées*, no. 552.

[136] See Pousset, *Life in Faith and Freedom*, p. 49.

[137] H. Rahner, *Ignatius*, p. 12.

[138] Margaret Silf, *Landmarks* (London: DLT, 2002), p. 103.

[139] William Barclay, *Epilogues and Prayers* (London: SCM Press, 1963), p. 98.

[140] See Francis de Sales, *Treatise on the Love of God*, ch. xi, no. 6, pp. 344. See http: //www.catholicspiritualdirection.org/treatiseloveofgod.pdf

[141] Guardini, *Prayers from Theology*, p. 53.

[142] John Bunyan, *The Pilgrim's Progress*, tr. Robert J. Edmonson, CJ (Mumbai: St Pauls, 2012.), p. 50.

[143] See www.luminarium. org/renlit/ moredevoutprayer.htm for this devout prayer of St Thomas More.

[144] Casey, *Toward God*, pp. 155-156.

[145] Pousset, *Life in Faith and Freedom*, p. 75.

[146] Pousset, *Life in Faith and Freedom*, p. 75.

[147] See Teilhard de Chardin, *The Prayer of the Universe* (London: Collins, Fontana Books, 1973), pp. 54-55.

[148] See Pousset, *Life in Faith and Freedom*, pp. 75-76.

[149] Laplace, *An Experience of Life in the Spirit*, p. 61.

[150] Roger Schütz (1915 – 2005), the founder of the ecumenical Taizé Community.

[151] Bernard, *Sermons on the Song of Songs* as in M. Casey, *Toward God*, p. 128 (third person changed to second).

[152] Brhadaranyaka Upanishad (I. iii. 28).

[153] See Bernard, *On the Song of Songs*, vol. III, ser. 57, nn. 7-8, as in Martin, *The Fulfilment of All Desire*, p. 354.

[154] Erich Przywara, *The Divine Majesty*, p. 54.

[155] Reprobus, a Canaanite of mighty stature, "took it into his head to seek out the greatest prince in the world, that he might serve and obey him." And he found one, a Christian King. Observing him making the sign of the cross at the mention of the Devil, he thought the Devil was greater than the King; so he went searching for the Devil and found him, a cruel and horrid figure, in a desert. So he began his service to the Devil till one day he found the Devil avoiding the symbol of a cross. Realizing there was someone greater than the Devil he found him to be the Christ who hung on the cross. So he became a Christian and was christened Christopher and served the kingly Christ as a hermit taught him! See *The Catholic Herald*, July 25, 2008, p. 14.

[156] Here is the kernel in the idea of kingship as remarked by K. Rahner, *Spiritual Exercises*, p. 129.

[157] See Pascal, *Pensées*, no. 792.

[158] See Cusson, *Biblical Theology and Spiritual Exercises*, p. 201.

[159] See González Dávila in his Directory as cited by Cusson p. 175.

[160] See Pousset, *Life in Faith and Freedom*, p. 64.

[161] H. Rahner, *Ignatius*, p. 108.

[162] Found in the Epistle of Barnabas cited in H. Rahner, *Ignatius*, p. 108.

[163] Karl Rahner, *Ignatius of Loyola*, pp. 26-27.

[164] A fourth-century desert Father with legendary fame venerated both in the West and the East to whom St Ignatius was attracted.

[165] As the charming legend has it, Rocamadour, meaning lover of the rock, goes back to Zacchaeus who had known Jesus. In history the name refers to a place of pilgrimage in France for a millennium. It stands as a witness to someone who chose to live alone with God.

[166] Alan Paton, *Instrument of Thy Peace* (New York: Newbury Press, 1968), p. 83.

[167] See Carroll Stuhlmueller in R. Brown, J. A. Fitzymer and R. E. Murphy, *The Jerome Biblical Commentary* (London: Geoffrey Chapman, 1970), n. 44:158, p. 158. Hereafter *Jerome Biblical Commentary*.

[168] Wm Paul Young, *The Shack* (Newbury Park, CA: Windblown Media, 2007), p. 183.

[169] Modified from Barclay, *Epilogues and Prayers*, p. 50.

[170] J. Laplace, *An Experience of Life in the Spirit*, p. 94.

[171] K. Rahner, *Spiritual Exercises*, p. 127.

[172] H. Rahner, *Ignatius*, p. 112.

[173] So St Gregory the Great. See *The Divine Office*, v. II, p. 554.

[174] K. Rahner, *Spiritual Exercises*, pp. 130-131.

[175] See Harvé Coathalem, *Ignatian Heights: A Guide to the Complete Exercises* (Taichung, Taiwan: Kuangchi Press, 1961), pp. 143-144.

[176] P. Divarkar, "Our Hearts Burning", in Series *Subsidia ad Exercitia*, n. 13, (Rome: 1975), p. 20.

[177] K. Rahner, *Ignatius of Loyola*, p. 20.

[178] M. Casey, *Toward God*, p. 148.

[179] Barclay, *Epilogues and Prayers*, p. 64 (slightly changed).

[180] Partly based on Peter A. Fraile, *God within Us* (Chicago, Ill: Loyola Univ. Press, 1986), pp. 43-45.

[181] Adapted from Elisabeth Allard, *Sayings of Jeanne Jugan* (Baltimore, MD: Little Sisters of the Poor, 2004), p. 17.

182 https://www.goodreads.com/author/quotes/24706.John Henry Newman (May 28, 2015).

183 See Elisabeth Allard, *Sayings of Jeanne Jugan*, pp. 30-31.

184 http://www.prudencetrue.com/images/TheLadderofDivineAscent.pdf Step 26, # 1, p. 89. St. John Climacus, *The Ladder of Divine Ascent*, tr. Archimandrite Lazarus Moore (Harper & Brothers, 1959).

185 K. Rahner, *Spiritual Exercises*, p. 22.

186 Anthony Buś, *A Mother's Plea* (Stockbridge, MA: Marian Press 2005), p. 19.

187 See Brian Grogan, *Way of Ignatius*, pp. 179-180.

188 *Pacé* the criticism of Newman's supposed failure to realize that "feeling is the deeper source of religion" by William James, *Varieties of Religious Experience* (New York, 1911), p. 431. Newman credited the effectiveness of Jesuits *of his time* to their practice of daily examen which is so much linked to feelings and discernment.

189 See MI II, 2, pp. 511, 682, 683 as in H. Rahner, *Ignatius*, pp. 139-140.

190 See H. Rahner, *Ignatius*, p. 144; Gerard W. Hughes, "Forgotten truths", in *Way of Ignatius*, p. 31.

191 See his own Directory in MI II, 2, p. 96 as in H. Rahner, *Ignatius*, p. 146.

192 See H. Rahner, *Ignatius*, pp. 144, 154.

193 An agraphon on which see H. Rahner, *Ignatius*, pp. 174-180.

194 So St Bernard too. See M. Casey, *Toward God*, p. 122.

195 See M. Basil Pennington, *Thomas Merton, Brother Monk* (San Francisco: Harper and Row, 1987), p. 19.

196 See Laplace, *An Experience of Life in the Spirit*, p. 97.

197 Egide van Broeckhoven, *A Friend to all Men*, p. 25.

198 Young, *The Shack*, p. 188 (with a change of capitals when referring to God).

199 See Guardini, *Prayers from Theology*, p. 37.

200 Guigo, *Scala Claustralium*, as in Simon Tugwell, *Ways of Imperfection* (Springfield, Il: Templegate Publishers, 1985), p. 96.

201 See Fraile, *God within Us*, p. 52.

202 Oliver Todd, *The Loyola Pilgrim* (Chelmsford Essex: Matthew James Pub. Ltd: 2003), p. 208.

203 See Lilly Zahrnke in her study of the spiritual sources of the *Exercises* as in H. Rahner, *Ignatius*, p. 193.

204 People like C. S. Lewis and Osho have said so. For example, the latter has said: "The art of disciplehood is the art of being a feminine consciousness" in his *Just Like That*, p. 5. www.osho.com/iosho/library/read-book?p...

205 St Augustine, *Confessions*, bk x, no. 27, p. 201.

206 See Peters, *The Spiritual Exercises of St Ignatius*, p. 119.

207 See Peters, *The Spiritual Exercises of St Ignatius*, p. 146.

208 Elisabeth Allard, *Sayings of Jeanne Jugan*, pp. 56, 60.

209 Such is the import of the word *philein* found, for example, at Mt 10:37.

210 Edmund Spenser, "Easter".

211 Alan Paton, *Instrument of Thy Peace*, p. 63.

212 See John L. McKenzie, *Dictionary of the Bible* (Bangalore: Asian Trading Corporation, 1998), p. 521.

213 Barclay, *Epilogues and Prayers*, p. 92.

214 See Peters, *The Spiritual Exercises of St Ignatius*, p. 118.

215 In a letter of Blessed Charles de Foucauld to his friend Duveyrier as in Antoine Chatelard, *Charles de Foucauld* (Bangalore: Claretian Publications, 2013), p. 61.

216 Following Bernard Lonergan; see William Johnston, *"Arise, My Love..."* *Mysticism for a New Era* (New York: Maryknoll, 2000), p. 39.

217 See Bruce Vawter in *Jerome Biblical Commentary*, n. 62:24, p. 410.

218 See Ramón Lull, *The Book of the Lover and Beloved*, tr. Allison Peers (Cambridge, Ontario: In Parentheses Publications, 2000), p. 4.

219 See Pousset, *Life in Faith and Freedom*, p. 18.

220 K. Rahner, *Ignatius of Loyola*, p. 21.

221 Pedro Arrupe, "Rooted and Grounded in Love", in *Companions in the Mission of Jesus* (Washington, D.C. : Georgetown University Press, 1987), pp. 29-30, the quotation being significantly the last paragraph in *Spiritual Exercises*.

222 See Johnston, *"Arise, My Love..."* *Mysticism for a New Era*, p. 17.

223 So St Augustine. See http://www.spck.org.uk/classic-prayers/st-augustine/

224 An anonymous Franciscan of 14th century, *Meditationes Vitae Christi* as in H. Rahner, *Ignatius*, p. 193.

225 See Pedro Arrupe, *Jesuit Apostolates Today* (Anand, India: GSP, 1981), p. 263.

226 Syren Kierkegaard, *Philosophical Fragments* (Princeton, NJ: Princeton Univ. Press, 1962), p. 131 as in John S. Dunne, *The Homing Spirit* (New York: Crossword, 1987), p. 20.

227 As Goethe wrote. See www.goodreads.com/quotes/23105

228 Osho, *Just Like That*, p. 63. See www.osho.com/iosho/library/read-book?p...

229 Hugo Rahner, *Saint Ignatius Loyola: Letters to Women* (Edinburgh-London: Nelson, 1960), p. 178.

230 H. Rahner, *Ignatius*, p. 185.

231 Thomas A Kempis, *The Imitation of Christ*, bk III, ch. 1.

232 See Jerome Nadal quoted in H. Rahner, *Ignatius*, p. 205.

233 See John of the Cross, *The Ascent of Mount Carmel*, tr. Allison Peers (New York: Image Books, 1958), bk I, ch. 11, no. 6, p. 63.

234 See Thomas Aquinas' Commentary on St John's Gospel in *The Divine Office*, v. III, pp. 156-157.

235 H. Rahner, *Ignatius*, p. 189.

236 H. Rahner, *Ignatius*, p. 189.

237 H. Rahner, *Ignatius*, p. 191.

238 Based on Hadewijch's *Levet God ende hi u ende ghi ons* (Live God's life, and He will be Yours, and you ours) as in Van Broeckhoven, *A Friend to All Men*, pp. 71, 117.

239 See Anthony Buś, *A Mother's Plea*, p. 53.

240 A petition in the prayer *Anima Christi* in the version known to St Ignatius. See H. Rahner, *Ignatius*, p. 121.

241 See Vatican Council II, *Gaudium et spes*, # 37.

242 See Cusson, *Biblical Theology and Spiritual Exercises*, p. 253.

243 See Cusson, *Biblical Theology and Spiritual Exercises*, pp. 255-256.

244 Anthony Buś, *A Mother's Plea*, p. 20.

245 As Teresa of Avila called it.

246 The Tamil word meaning Yes.

247 St Augustine, *Confessions*, bk xiii, no. 9, p. 278.

248 Source unknown. See http://www.champagnat.org/401.php?a=6&id=1979

249 Cusson, *Biblical Theology and Spiritual Exercises*, pp. 260-261.

250 See Cusson, *Biblical Theology and Spiritual Exercises*, p. 262.

251 So Madeleine Delbrêl (1904–1964) writing in her religious maturity as a Catholic Christian right in the midst of continuous social service and acute sensitivity towards people after a youth spent as a strict atheist. See C. Martini, *The Ignatian Exercises in the Light of St John* (Anand: GSP, 1981), p. 95.

252 See Ganss, *The Spiritual Exercises*, pp. 174-175; also Bernard, *On the Song of Songs*, vol. II, ser. 42, n. 9, p. 217 as in R. Martin, pp. 247-248.

253 See M. Casey, *Toward God*, p. 165.

254 Adapted from Elisabeth Allard, *Sayings of Jeanne Jugan*, pp. 42-43.

255 http://www.prudencetrue.com/images/TheLadderofDivineAscent.pdf Step 25, # 41, p. 87.

256 Buś, *A Mother's Plea*, p. 138.

257 As Golda Meir, a former Prime Minister of Israel, said.

258 Josef Sellmair, *The Priest in the World*, p. 79.

[259] See K. Rahner, *Ignatius of Loyola*, p. 22.

[260] See C. S. Lewis, *Surprised by Joy*, pp. 228-229. Etty Hillesum wrote movingly: "A desire to kneel down sometimes pulses through my body, or rather it is as if my body had been meant and made for the act of kneeling. Sometimes, in moments of deep gratitude, kneeling down becomes an overwhelming urge, head deeply bowed, hands before my face. It has become a gesture embedded in my body, needing to be expressed from time to time.... When I write these things down, I still feel a little ashamed, as if I were writing about the most intimate of intimate matters. Much more bashful than if I had to write about my love life. But is there indeed anything as intimate as humanity's relationship to God?" as in Pleshoyano, *The Way*, p. 15.

[261] K. Rahner, *Spiritual Exercises*, p. 202 .

[262] The inscription on her tomb. See http://www.loretodelhi.com/our_founder.aspx

[263] See *Martin Luther King in My Own Words*, selected by C. S. King (London: Hodder & Stoughton, 2002), p. 44.

[264] Young, *The Shack*, p. 180.

[265] http://www.prudencetrue.com/images/TheLadderofDivineAscent.pdf Step 28, # 29, p. 122.

[266] St Albert the Albert, *On Cleaving to God* (Sublime Books, 2014), p.6.

[267] Pousset, *Life in Faith and Freedom*, p. 60.

[268] See Pousset, *Life in Faith and Freedom*, pp. 57-63.

[269] Buś, *A Mother's Plea*, p. 123.

[270] http://www.prudencetrue.com/images/TheLadderofDivineAscent.pdf Step 28, # 29, p. 122 (with a slight change).

[271] See the letter of St Ignatius to Inés Pascual in *Obras Completas*, 613 as in Timothy M. Gallagher, *The Examen Prayer* (New York: Crossword, 2006), p. 58.

[272] See S. H. Hooke, *The Resurrection of Christ* (London: DLT, 1967), p. 135.

[273] A prayer of St Benedict in *The Lourdes Pilgrim*, p. 214.

[274] See Ladilaus Boros, *God is With Us*, p. 2.

[275] A cross-cultural experience, though not universal, as I have come across Indians with no such experience. See C. S. Lewis, *Four Loves* (London: Collins, Fount Paperbacks, 1984), p. 88.

[276] Even non-Christians, like Osho, speak of Jesus in such terms; see his *Just Like That*, p. 3. See www.osho.com/iosho/library/read-book?p...

[277] Catherine of Siena, *The Dialogue*, p. 193.

[278] See *The Spiritual Canticle*, Stanza xv, p. 12 in *The Collected Works of John of the Cross*, p. 412.

[279] Pousset, *Life in Faith and Freedom*, p. 146.

[280] See Pousset, *Life in Faith and Freedom* (slightly changed).

[281] Pousset, *Life in Faith and Freedom*, p. 144.

[282] J. Guillet, *Jesus Christ Yesterday and Today* (Chicago, 1965), p. 156 as in Cusson, *Biblical Theology and Spiritual Exercises*, p. 294.

[283] See www.luminarium.org/renlit/moredevoutprayer.htm for this prayer of St Thomas More

[284] See P. Divarkar, "Our Hearts are Burning", *Subsidia*, n. 13, p. 21.

[285] See Dag Hammarskjöld, *Markings*, p. 33.

[286] So Dionysius the Areopagite. See Dávila, MI II, 2, p. 526 cited in H. Rahner, *Ignatius*, p. 132.

[287] As it has for some; see e.g., *Martin Luther King in My Own Words*, p. 78.

[288] See www.luminarium.org/renlit/moredevoutprayer.htm for this prayer of St Thomas More.

[289] See *The Gospel of Sri Ramakrishna* (New York: Ramakrishna-Vivekananda Centre, 1980), as in Johnston, *"Arise, My Love..." Mysticism for a New Era*, p. 41 (with slight changes).

[290] Pousset, *Life in Faith and Freedom*, p. 154.

[291] Keats, *Sleep and Poetry*, lines 123-125.

[292] See Elisabeth Allard, *Sayings of Jeanne Jugan*, pp. 70-71.

[293] A prayer of Gerald O'Mahony in *Let Justice Roll Down*, compiled by Geoffrey Duncan (Norwich: Canterbury Press, 2003), p. 177.

[294] See Guardini, *Prayers from Theology*, p. 44.

[295] Pousset, *Life in Faith and Freedom*, p. 154.

[296] H. U. von Balthasar, *Prayer*, p. 241 as in Dermot Mansfield, "Praying the Passion", in *Way of Ignatius*, pp. 110-111.

[297] Based on St Augustine, Sermo 27, 6 as in H. Rahner, *Ignatius*, p. 133.

[298] Like Plato, for example; see Laplace, *An Experience of Life in the Spirit*, p. 88.

[299] Based on St Ignatius; see MI I, 1, p. 502 as in H. Rahner, *St Ignatius*, p. 133.

[300] Gerard W. Hughes, *Oh, God, Why?* (Oxford: Bible Reading Fellowship, 1993), p. 133.

[301] See Michael de la Bedoyere, *Francis de Sales* (New York: Harper and Bros, 1960), p. 193.

[302] Rousseau echoing the Roman centurion in this fashion, http://www.bartleby.com/ 348/225.html (accessed 28 May 2015).

[303] See H. Rahner, *St Ignatius*, pp. 130-131.

[304] See Guardini, *Prayers from Theology*, p. 38.

[305] Elisabeth Allard, *Sayings of Jeanne Jugan*, p. 85.

[306] Davila, MI II, 2, p. 526 as in H. Rahner, *St Ignatius*, pp. 131-132.

[307] See Hughes, *Oh, God, Why?*, p. 113.

[308] In Japanese *Mu ni naru*. For an example of its practice see Johnston, *"Arise, My Love..." Mysticism for a New Era*, p. 106.

[309] Macquarrie, *The Humility of God* (London: SCM, 1978), p. 59 (with slight changes).

[310] See Przywara, *The Divine Majesty*, pp. 71-72.

[311] See Ramón Lull, *The Book of the Lover and Beloved*, p. 18.

[312] See Peters, *Spiritual Exercises of St Ignatius*, p. 117.

[313] Macquarrie, *The Humility of God*, p. 60.

[314] Peters, *Spiritual Exercises of St Ignatius*, p. 144.

[315] See Dunne, *The Homing Spirit*, p. 18.

[316] Adapted from from Elisabeth Allard, *Sayings of Jeanne Jugan*, p. 85.

[317] Guigo, *Scala Claustralium*, as in Simon Tugwell, *Ways of Imperfection*, p. 95.

[318] See Cusson, *Biblical Theology and Spiritual Exercises*, p. 308.

[319] From the devout prayer of St Thomas More. See www. luminarium. org/ renlit/ moredevoutprayer.htm

[320] See Jeffrey Cave in Francis B. Sayre Jr, *To Stand in the Cross* (New York: Seabury Press, 1978), p. 63.

[321] To use John Milton, *Samson Agonistes*.

[322] From a sermon of St Ephraem as in *The Divine Office*, v. III, p. 45*.

[323] See Peters, *Spiritual Exercises of St Ignatius*, pp. 145-146.

[324] See the comparison of the way exercitants emerge in the different Weeks in Peters, *Spiritual Exercises*, p. 147.

[325] Bach's Cantata no. 147.

[326] Cusson, *Biblical Theology and Spiritual Exercises*, p. 305.

[327] See Cusson, *Biblical Theology and Spiritual Exercises*, p. 318.

[328] See M. Casey, *Toward God*, pp. 160, 163.

[329] So Augustine quoted in *The Book of Privy Counselling*, ch. 13.

[330] See Guardini, *Prayers from Theology*, p. 37.

[331] St Bernard as in M. Casey, *Toward God*, p. 128.

[332] Like blind flying with the help of instruments though without being able to see, blind seeing is seeing with a higher power what is not available to usual vision.

[333] Bruce Vawter in *Jerome Biblical Commentary*, n. 63:178, p. 464.

[334] Slightly changed from Gerald O'Mahony, *Do Not Be Afraid* (Suffolk: Kevin Mayhew, 1999), p. 92.

[335] See the devout prayer of St Thomas More. See www. luminarium. org/renlit/ moredevoutprayer.htm

336 http://hillconnections.org/rr/celebrating-Gods-gifts-with-Hildegard-of-Bingen-12st.pdf (accessed 28-615)

337 Teilhard de Chardin, *The Prayer of the Universe*, (London: Collins Fontana 1973), pp. 137-138.

338 Radcliffe, *What is the Point of Being Christian?* (London: Burns and Oates, 2006), pp. 52-53.

339 So St Ignatius in a letter; see MI I, 2, p. 510 as cited in H. Rahner, *Ignatius*, p. 135.

340 http://archive.org/stream/raymondlullillum00barbuoft/raymondlullillum00barbuoft_djvu.txt

341 See Henri J. M. Nouwen, *The Return of the Prodigal Son* (London: DLT, 1994), p.116.

342 Seen in the Crucifix in the house of St Francis Xavier; reported long before by Julian of Norwich.

343 See Erich Przywara, *The Divine Majesty*, p. 56.

344 Adapted from Elisabeth Allard, *Sayings of Jeanne Jugan*, p. 62.

345 See Bernard Lonergan, *Insight* (London, 1958), p. 699.

346 To use the phrase of Heraclitus.

347 Teilhard de Chardin at Peking on Oct 20, 1945 as in de Lubac, *The Faith of Teilhard de Chardin*, p. 28.

348 St Angela of Foligno as in de Lubac, *The Faith of Teilhard de Chardin*, p. 26.

349 Adapted from Guardini, *Prayers from Theology*, p. 26.

350 H. Rahner, *Ignatius*, p. 9.

351 Martin Heidegger in Dunne, *The Homing Spirit*, pp. 12-13.

352 As the early Church Fathers wrote.

353 So a Jewish writer as in Hughes, *Oh, God, Why?*, p. 49.

354 See H. Rahner, *Ignatius*, p. 6 .

355 See G. Gispert-Sauch, "Experiencing the deeper self", *Ignis*, 2004, no. 2, p. 42.

356 See Young, *The Shack*, pp. 206-207.

357 A prayer of Ludwig von Beethoven as in Thomas Nelson, *Table Graces for the Family* (Nashville, Tennessee: W Publishing Group, 2005), p. 43.

358 As in the Letter to the Whole Society (12 April 2010) of Fr General A. Nicolás for the Beatification of Fr Bernardo de Hojos.

359 See Elisabeth Allard, *Sayings of Jeanne Jugan*, p. 84.

360 See Elisabeth Allard, *Sayings of Jeanne Jugan*, pp. 64, 73-74.

361 From the devout prayer of St Thomas More. See www. luminarium. org/ renlit/ moredevoutprayer.htm

362 Dante Alighieri (1265–1321), *Paradiso*, Canto XXIII, line 145 (the very last line of his *Divine Comedy*).

363 Grogan, "The one who gives the Exercises", *Way of Ignatius*, pp. 180-181.

364 St Anselm in Barclay, *Epilogues and Prayers*, p. 195.

365 Karl Rahner, *Theological Investigations* III (London, 67), 297-298 as in H. Rahner, *Ignatius*, pp. 208-209.

366 Despite the self-acknowledged restraint in expressions of tenderness Nerea Alzola, "Women helping to give the Spiritual Exercises", *The Way*, 49/1 (January 2010), p. 55.

367 So Nadal about Ignatius; see P. Leturia, "Genesis de la Ejercicios", *Archivum historicum Societatis Jesu*, X (1941), pp. 56-57 as in H. Rahner, *The Spirituality of St Ignatius Loyola* (Chicago: Loyola University Press: 1980), p. 98.

368 See John of the Cross, *The Ascent of Mount Carmel*, bk II, ch. 20, no. 3, pp. 185-186.

AFTERWORD

During the Spiritual Exercises when a person is seeking God's will, it is more appropriate and far better that the Creator and Lord himself should communicate himself to the devout soul, embracing it in love and praise, and disposing it for the way which will enable the soul to serve him better in the future. Accordingly the one giving the Exercises ought not to lean or incline in either direction but rather, while standing like the pointer of a scale in equilibrium, to allow the Creator to deal immediately with the creature and the creature with its Creator and Lord.

While pondering God of the Exercises by A. Paul Dominic SJ this annotation to the Exercises (# 15) which is meant to guide directors came to mind. Being invited into his colloquy of prayer at dawn, morning and evening offers the reader a unique opportunity to enter into a director's desires to be with, to be immersed in the God activity of the Exercises. For anyone who has directed the Exercises it becomes paramount to pray for our exercitants but also to pray the impact of the Exercises upon our lives at the time we are giving them. Having recently completed accompanying someone in the full individually directed "30 day retreat", I resonate with the joy, the commitment and the changing moments in our own relationship with God as we direct others.

I find particularly moving those moments in the diary when God, Jesus, the Spirit and Mary respond to Paul's offering or questioning or pleading. The touch of God with us, Mary journeying with us makes vivid and real how significant and important that touch can be for the director and needs to be for the exercitant. Paul mentions infrequently how the three-fold prayer of each day reveals itself in those he directed. I would have welcomed more of that revelation without violating confidentiality of course.

I will call back into memory the gifts I have received
—my creation, redemption, and the other gifts particular to myself.
I will ponder with deep affection how much our God has done for me,
and how much he has given me of what he possesses,
and consequently how he, the same Lord, desires to give me
even his very self, in accordance with his divine design. (# 234)

The great gift of the Spiritual Exercises to the churches and to the world is their promise of renewed inner freedom rooted in a conversion of mind, heart and spirit, rooted in being chosen by Christ for his mission in the Church and within societies. Ignatius shapes the Exercises from his own conversion journey and as such the power and dynamic grace of the Exercises transcends time, space, and culture while needing to be adapted to the changing realities of theology, psychology and societal roles of women and men.

Paul reveals how the gift of directing the Exercises calls upon all of us to be willing to have our hearts changed, to recognize the gift of God given at each moment of this journey, to see with new eyes the realities of our lives and cultures. It is clear that Paul's prayer changed him over the dawning days and nights of this retreat. I imagine because of the assiduous commitment to notice what God was/is doing in him that his way of seeing God, Jesus, Spirit and Mary in his exercitants was changed as well.

Fr. Paul and I have only met via technology. There would be much more I would like to explore with him about his retreat prayer if we did not live continents away. He leaves me with the gift of being very attentive to my own prayer as I have been but will do in a new way because of his book based on his own journey. May this book inspire all of us called to this ministry to recognize the gift of God in our calling.

The Poet Michael F. Suarez in Jesuit Studies reminds us:

The giver is the gift
again the giver is present, undiminished.

the giver is without limits,
love universal, but always specific.

prizing everything precious,
as it is.

Disbuild the tower you have raised
scatter the treasure you have saved

forget the points you'd thought you earned
for good behaviour.

The giver is the gift of worth:
you do not get what you deserve.

May the gift of these reflective prayers remind each one of us exercitants and accompaniers that the GIVER IS THE GIFT !

Nancy Y. Sheridan SASV

Nancy Y Sheridan SASV has been involved in directing the Spiritual Exercises of St. Ignatius for over twenty years. She has been a collaborator of the New England Province of the Society of Jesus as a member of the staff at Eastern Point Retreat House in Gloucester, MA and on the team of the Center for Religious Development in Cambridge, MA USA. She has been an adjunct faculty member at Weston Jesuit School of Theology in the area of Spirituality and in that capacity taught with Fr. Thomas Hamel SJ, William Devine SJ, David Donovan SJ and Kenneth J. Hughes SJ courses on the Spiritual Exercises as well as an experiential reading of *The Reminiscences of St. Ignatius.* She has directed retreats in the USA, Canada, Ireland, and soon in Wales. She supervised and directed numerous Indian Jesuits in the course of this journey.